**This Book Comes With Lots of
FREE Online Resources**

Get more family law information on Nolo's award-winning website. Here you can:

GET DISCOUNTS ON NOLO PRODUCTS – Get discounts on hundreds of books, forms, and software

READ BLOGS – Get the latest info from Nolo authors' blogs

LISTEN TO PODCASTS – Listen to authors discuss timely issues on topics that interest you

WATCH VIDEOS – Get a quick introduction to a topic with our short videos

And that's not all. Nolo.com contains thousands of articles on everyday legal and business issues, plus a plain-English law dictionary, all written by Nolo experts and available for free. You'll also find more useful **books, software, online apps, downloadable forms,** plus a **lawyer directory.**

Second Abridged Edition

The Legal Answer Book for Families

Attorney Emily Doskow & Marcia Stewart

SECOND ABRIDGED
EDITION   AUGUST 2014

Editor   LINA GUILLEN

Cover Design   SUSAN PUTNEY

Book Design   TERRI HEARSH

Proofreading   IRENE BARNARD

Index   BAYSIDE INDEXING

Printing   BANG PRINTING

ISBN: 978-1-4133-2085-5

This book covers only United States law, unless it specifically states otherwise.

Please note

We believe accurate, plain-English legal information should help
you solve many of your own legal problems. But this text is not a
substitute for personalized advice from a knowledgeable lawyer.
If you want the help of a trained professional—and we'll always
point out situations in which we think that's a good idea—
consult an attorney licensed to practice in your state.

Acknowledgments

We couldn't have written this book without our editors Lina Guillen and Mary Randolph. Every page reflects their outstanding editing and writing skills and great ideas. Special thanks to Stephen Stine and Charlie Walmann for invaluable help assembling and updating the appendix of 50-state rules and resources. Thanks also to the many Nolo editors and authors who contributed material to this book, especially our editor and family law specialist Lina Guillen, but also: Mary Randolph (wills and estate planning); Ilona Bray (immigration issues affecting families and children); Diana Fitzpatrick (family-related tax issues); Lisa Guerin (employment laws affecting minors); Beth Laurence and Betsy Simmons Hannibal (elder care); David Goguen (alcohol and other laws affecting children); and Micah Schwartzbach and Janet Portman (juvenile justice and education).

About the Authors

Emily Doskow is a practicing attorney and mediator who has worked with families in the Bay Area for more than 20 years. She is the author of *Nolo's Essential Guide to Divorce* and *Nolo's Essential Guide to Child Custody and Support* and a coauthor of *The Sharing Solution: How to Save Money, Simplify Your Life & Build Community* (with Janelle Orsi) and *Making It Legal: A Guide to Same-Sex Marriage, Domestic Partnerships & Civil Unions* (with Frederick Hertz). Emily is also editor of many Nolo titles including *Divorce After 50: A Guide to the Unique Legal & Financial Challenges*, *Divorce Without Court: A Guide to Mediation & Collaborative Divorce,* and the best-selling *Neighbor Law: Fences, Trees, Boundaries & Noise*. Emily specializes in family law, including adoption, parentage issues, dissolution of same-sex and opposite-sex relationships, and mediation and collaborative divorce. She is a graduate of the Boalt Hall School of Law at the University of California at Berkeley.

Marcia Stewart has written and edited dozens of Nolo books on a wide range of topics affecting families, from special education to house buying to Social Security.

Table of Contents

Your Family Legal Companion

Questions about our families and the law pop up all the time. Where can I get a copy of my child's birth certificate? How much child support will I have to pay if I get divorced? Where can I get help finding and financing long-term care for my older parents?

Finding the answers isn't always easy, even in the age of instant online information. Laws affecting couples, children, and families vary from state to state. Online resources are often out of date or too general. Sure, lawyers can tell us, but obviously it's not practical to dash off to a lawyer every time something comes up.

That's why we wrote this book. Use it to find quick answers to a wide variety of practical questions you might have about how the law (federal, state, and local) affects you and your family. We'll tell you what kinds of legal matters you can handle on your own and when it makes sense to hire a lawyer—for example, if you're going through a contested divorce or your teenager is charged with a criminal offense.

This book is for people in any kind of family. If you have children or are thinking of having or adopting them, or are getting married or divorced (or thinking of doing so), you're bound to have legal and financial questions. If you're planning for your own senior years or helping a parent plan, questions about government benefits are almost inevitable. If you're with a same-sex partner, the laws seem to be changing every week—

Find Your State Rules and Other Family Law Resources at Nolo.com

Throughout this book we provide carefully chosen lists of websites, government agencies, and nonprofit organizations that offer the best information on specific legal issues affecting families—from adoption to elder care. For state-specific information, see the Divorce & Family Law section of Nolo's website (www.nolo.com/legal-encyclopedia/family-law-divorce). This contains links to state court information, family law forms (such as divorce forms you can fill out yourself), and statutes, plus state-by-state information on a wide range of topics, including marriage requirements, grounds for divorce, and child support guidelines.

If you're looking for federal and local laws that affect your family or advice on doing your own research, see the Legal Research section of Nolo's website (www.nolo.com/legal-research).

The Nolo website also has a wide variety of free articles, FAQs, blogs, podcasts, videos, and more on many legal topics affecting families, plus hundreds of do-it-yourself books for sale (both print and eBook versions) and downloadable forms, on topics such as estate planning, immigration, late-life divorce, debt and credit, and family leave.

Finally, if you need an attorney, Nolo's Lawyer Directory (www.nolo.com/lawyers) will help you find one in your area. Nolo's directory provides a detailed profile for each attorney listed, with information about the lawyer's experience, education, fees, and general philosophy of practicing law.

in this book, you'll find out the latest developments (and information about how to stay up to date). In other words, whether you have a question about a newborn or a teenager, a house full of kids or an empty nest, a parent or a spouse, *The Legal Answer Book for Families* has something for you. It's the ultimate resource for commonly asked questions about creating and protecting families. ●

Marriage

We think of marriage as a romantic institution, but it's also a legal arrangement—a contract, really, with terms written by the state. Most people enter into that contract with no real idea of what those terms are. Most people planning to get married haven't considered how a prenuptial agreement works, and most newlyweds (or not-so-newlyweds) don't know what marriage means in terms of sharing a spouse's property, income, and debts. Things get even murkier if your fiancé is from another country or you're in a same-sex relationship. Here are some of the basics about marriage and marriage-like relationships.

STATE RULES

State marriage rules. The Marriage & Relationships section of Nolo's website (www.nolo.com/legal-encyclopedia/marriage) contains state rules on marriage license requirements, same-sex marriage, common law marriage, and more.

The Legal Rights and Benefits of Marriage

Married couples receive numerous rights and benefits under both federal and state law. These include:

- income tax benefits, such as the ability to transfer property between spouses with no tax consequences
- inheritance rights to a deceased spouse's property
- government benefits, such as Social Security spousal retirement and death benefits

- employment benefits, such as the right to take medical leave to care for a spouse who becomes ill
- the right to make medical decisions if your spouse is incapacitated and to make decisions about body disposal and organ donation
- financial support, including equitable property division and the right to seek alimony in a divorce
- the ability to sponsor your spouse for a green card
- the right to leave your spouse unlimited amounts of money not subject to the federal estate tax
- protection from having to testify against your spouse in a court proceeding, and
- consumer benefits, such as family rates for various types of insurance.

These are just a few of the benefits that come with marriage. Some of them—the ones that are governed by state law—also apply to same-sex couples who are legally married or are in domestic partnerships or civil unions in marriage-equivalent states. Now that a key provision of the federal Defense of Marriage Act (DOMA) has been overturned, legally married same-sex couples will qualify for federal benefits just as opposite-sex married couples do. However, eligibility rules vary among federal agencies. Some agencies will recognize all legally valid same-sex marriages, regardless of where married couples live. Others, such as the Social Security Administration, use the "place of domicile" rule, which means that married couples must live in a state that recognizes same-sex marriage in order to qualify for benefits. This means that same-sex spouses living in a non-recognition state, such as Texas, will not qualify for Social Security benefits based on their spouses' work records.

Getting Married: Rules, Licenses, and Ceremonies

Whether you're planning a wedding in a church or another religious venue, at city hall, on the beach, or in Las Vegas, you must follow the same basic rules.

Who Can Get Married

Only opposite-sex couples may get married in all but 19 states and the District of Columbia. The exceptions are discussed below, in "Same-Sex Marriage."

Other rules vary slightly from state to state, but here are the essentials:

- Each person must be at least the age of consent, which is usually 18. Younger people may be able to marry with their parents' consent.
- The intended spouses cannot be too closely related, such as siblings, aunts or uncles, or nieces or nephews, or, in some states, first cousins.
- Both people must have the mental capacity to understand what they are doing and its consequences.
- The parties must be sober at the time of the marriage.
- Neither party can be married to someone else.
- The couple must get a marriage license.

You do not need to be a legal resident of a state to be married there, although there is usually a residency requirement for divorce.

Marriage Licenses and Certificates

A marriage *license* is the piece of paper that authorizes you to get married before the fact, while a marriage *certificate* is the document that proves you are married once the wedding ceremony is over. Following are the typical steps couples take to get married.

Get the license from the appropriate city or county official, such as the county clerk, in the state where you want to be married. You'll need some kind of identification, and you might also need to bring a birth certificate or divorce decree. There's a fee for the license (usually $25 to $100, depending on the state and county), and licenses are good for 30 days to one year, depending on the state.

Will It Hurt to Get Married? Required Blood Tests

The vast majority of states do not require premarriage blood tests to check for sexually transmitted diseases (STDs) in both partners, and to see whether or not the bride to be has immunity to rubella, which can cause problems during pregnancy. The tests may also disclose the presence of genetic disorders, such as sickle-cell anemia or Tay-Sachs disease. No states require HIV tests, but some give out information about HIV and AIDS. In most states, blood tests aren't required for people over 50 or if someone is pregnant or sterile. If either partner tests positive for an STD, what then happens depends on the state. Some states may refuse to issue a marriage license.

Have a ceremony. Depending on the state, there may be a short waiting period (usually just a few days) between getting a license and getting married.

Get the marriage certificate. Most states require both spouses, the person who officiated, and one or two witnesses to sign the marriage certificate; often this is done just after the ceremony. Then the person who performed the ceremony must file the certificate with the appropriate county office (for example, the county clerk's office) where you live. A few weeks after getting the marriage certificate, the county sends the newlyweds a certified copy of the marriage certificate.

Marriage Ceremonies

A wedding ceremony may be nonreligious (civil) or religious. Civil ceremonies must be performed by a judge, justice of the peace, or court clerk who has legal authority to perform marriages, or by a person given temporary authority by a judge or court clerk. Religious ceremonies must be conducted by a clergy member—for example, a priest, minister, or rabbi. Some states have programs—like California's "deputy for a day" system—that allow a nonclergy friend or relative to officiate at a wedding. There's also the Universal Life Church, which will ordain anyone over the Internet, but the organization has occasionally run into legal problems over the validity of the ordinations (and therefore the marriages performed by the Universal Life ministers).

Usually, no special words are required as long as the spouses acknowledge their intention to marry each other—

once you've included that, you can design whatever type of ceremony you want.

Changing Your Name After Marriage

No law requires you to change your name just because you get married, though many people do.

If you want to take your new spouse's name, promptly and consistently begin to use that name. A court procedure isn't required, but it still takes some time and effort to change your name.

Some institutions will accept your marriage certificate as proof of your name change. Others require a government-issued form of identification in your new name, so it's a good idea to change your name with the Social Security Administration (SSA) first. Visit www.ssa.gov to download the required application form, or call the SSA at 800-772-1213. Then mail or take the completed application—along with your marriage certificate and proof of your identity—to a local Social Security office. A few weeks later, you will receive your new Social Security card, and you can begin to change your name with other institutions.

The big bureaucracies will take the longest to process your request, so you'll want to get the ball rolling with your state motor vehicle agency (usually called DMV) and the U.S. passport office. Then you can dive into the long list of other businesses and organizations in your life—banks, insurance agencies, health care practitioners, the voter registration office, employers, clubs, utilities, publications, and so on. You'll also need to update your personal documents, such as your will, living trust, or health care directive.

RESOURCE

For more information on changing your name, see www.nolo.com/legal-encyclopedia/name-change.

Sharing a Spouse's Debts, Property, and Income

How you will share and, if you divorce, divide the debts, property, and income that you and your spouse accrue after marriage depends mostly on where you live—specifically, whether your state follows community property rules or the common law system of dealing with marital property.

Common Law Property States

The majority of states (all but the community property states listed below) follow "common law" (also known as equitable distribution) property rules. In these states, debts incurred by one spouse in that spouse's name alone are usually that spouse's debts alone. However, a debt is owed by both spouses if it was:

- for a family necessity, such as food or shelter for the family or tuition for the kids

- jointly undertaken—for example, if both spouses' names are on an account or on the title to a house, or
- the debt was incurred fro medical purposes (in some states only).

All other debts, such as a business debt from one spouse's business, are considered the separate debt of the owner spouse—and generally a creditor cannot go after the income or property of the other spouse to collect.

Property also generally belongs to the spouse who earns it or whose name is on the title document. In most common law states, all of the following are separate property:

- income earned by one spouse, if it's kept separate (if it's mixed with the other spouse's money, it can be nearly impossible to tell what belongs to whom)
- property bought with one spouse's separate income or funds, unless the title to the property (such as a car) is put in both spouses' names
- gifts and inheritances received by one spouse, and
- property owned by one spouse before marriage (and kept separate).

Community Property States

In community property states, all of the income earned and property acquired, as well as all debts incurred, belong to both spouses together. (Together, the spouses are called "the community.") Couples who prefer to keep some or all of their debts and income separate can do so by signing a prenuptial agreement (discussed below).

Community Property States			
Alaska*	Idaho	New Mexico	Washington
Arizona	Louisiana	Texas	Wisconsin
California	Nevada		

* In Alaska, spouses can sign an agreement making specific assets community property.

Most debts incurred by one spouse during the marriage are owed by both spouses, even if only one spouse signed the paperwork for the debt. Debts incurred before marriage, such as a student loan, don't automatically become joint debts. However, a creditor can come after community property funds if the person who owes the debt fails to pay it. For example, if your spouse defaults on a student loan, the lender can try to collect from your joint accounts, even if you earned most of the money that's in those accounts.

All income earned by either spouse during marriage, as well as property bought with that income, is community property, owned equally by the spouses. Even if the spouse who earns income keeps the money in a separate account, that money still belongs to the other spouse too. However, money and property that the spouses owned before marriage are considered separate property as long as they're kept in the name of the person who owned them and not mixed up with the community money. It's common, however, for spouses to mix their money together once they marry, making it nearly impossible to tell what might still be separate property.

Gifts and inheritances received by one spouse are the separate property of that spouse.

Also, when one spouse owns a business that was started before the marriage, the business is considered that spouse's separate property—but the income generated by the business is community property, and the community often acquires an interest in the business itself because of increases in its value or because the nonowner spouse contributed work or ideas to it during the marriage.

How Marriage Affects Your Credit— and How to Avoid Problems

Many couples assume that a new, merged credit record is created when they marry. But, in fact, every credit record is tied to a single Social Security number. That means that your credit record, and any credit report you get, stays separate from your spouse's.

Both credit records do, however, list accounts that you and your spouse open jointly; list accounts with one of you named as cosigner; and reflect the addition of a spouse to an existing account as either a joint account holder or an authorized user.

How One Spouse's Credit Report Affects the Other's

When you and your spouse apply jointly for credit, a rental home, or insurance, both of your credit histories will be considered. If either one of you has unfavorable information in

your credit report, it will hurt your chances of getting credit—
or at least getting it at a good rate.

Ways to Hold Credit

When you're married, you have four choices when it comes
to applying for credit: (1) apply individually, (2) apply jointly,
(3) make one spouse a cosigner for the other, or (4) make
one spouse an authorized user but not a joint account holder.
Which one is best depends on the circumstances.

Individual Credit

One way to avoid trouble is to apply for credit individually—
that is, without your spouse. Of course, this strategy works only
if your income and assets alone are substantial enough to qualify
you for the credit. Qualifying on one income can be particularly
difficult when applying for a large loan, such as a mortgage.

If you live in a community property state, as a practical
matter it may be difficult to get a large loan on your own;
lenders generally insist that couples apply together, because
both spouses are responsible for the debt no matter who
applies for it. If your spouse's credit record is bad, the lender
may be reluctant to lend to you in the belief that your spouse's
bad financial habits will make you less likely to be able to pay
off the debt.

If you live in a common law state and you take out a loan
in your own name using only your own credit record, you're
the only person responsible for paying it back. If you don't pay
the loan, you're the only one whose credit will be damaged.

Joint Accounts

If you and your spouse are joint account holders, you are both liable for the debt. If you open a new account, each of you is legally responsible for repaying the entire debt. (And remember, if you live in a community property state, you may be liable even if your name isn't on the account.)

If one spouse adds the other to an existing account, the credit history—positive or negative—of the person with the existing account will affect that of the spouse who is added to the account. For example, if you have a positive credit history and add your spouse as a joint account holder to your existing account, your positive credit history will be factored into your spouse's score. If you have poor credit and add your spouse, your spouse's credit score will be harmed.

Adding your spouse to your account as a joint account holder will not affect your credit score unless your spouse uses much or all of your available credit.

Cosigners

Someone who cosigns for a debt becomes fully responsible for that debt if the primary borrower does not pay. Usually, lenders require a cosigner only if they're concerned that the borrower won't be able to pay. If your spouse has bad credit and a lender wants a cosigner, do it only if you are prepared to make payments if necessary.

Remember that if you are in a community property state, you are probably going to be liable for your spouse's debts even if you are not a cosigner.

Authorized User

If one spouse has poor credit, an alternative to applying for credit jointly is to designate that spouse as an authorized user on the other spouse's credit account. That way the less-qualified spouse can use the credit but is not liable for the debt (again, unless you're in a community property state).

Making one spouse an authorized user will not effect the account holder's credit score unless the authorized user uses much or all of the available credit—using up a large percentage of one's available credit has a negative effect on a person's credit rating. And, if the more solvent spouse decides later to remove the other from the account, it is much easier than if both were joint account holders.

If one spouse becomes an authorized user on the other's account, the account will appear on the authorized user's credit report. It may or may not affect his or her credit score.

How to Improve a Spouse's Bad Credit Record

Bad credit is not an insurmountable problem, but it can take time to turn things around. If you have excellent credit, you can help your spouse by:

- adding your spouse to one or more of your existing accounts (do this only if you are convinced your spouse will not charge up your balance)
- helping to pay down your spouse's balances, particularly if they are closer to the credit limit than yours are
- transferring your spouse's debt to one of your lower-interest accounts

- taking over bill paying if your spouse has spending or money management problems
- setting financial goals together, and
- checking your credit reports annually.

RESOURCE

More about maintaining good credit and repairing bad credit. The Bankruptcy section of Nolo.com includes lots of useful articles on debt and credit, including the basics of credit reports, and the Personal Finance section includes articles on budgeting and money management.

Prenuptial Agreements

A prenuptial or premarital agreement ("prenup") is a written contract created by a couple in anticipation of getting married, for the purpose of defining each person's financial rights and responsibilities. Typically, a prenup lists each person's property and debts and specifies what each person's property rights will be if the couple divorces. Without a prenup, state law controls how property is divided at divorce.

What You Can—and Cannot— Do With a Prenup

Prenups have commonly been used by very wealthy people to protect assets, but couples of more modest means are increasingly turning to them. Prenups can be used to:

- keep finances separate and clarify financial rights and responsibilities during marriage by stating who owns income earned and property acquired during marriage
- clarify ownership of and interests in a spouse's business
- create a plan for how property will be divided in the event of divorce
- decide on (in most states) alimony or spousal support in case of divorce
- state intentions regarding an estate plan and waive inheritance rights
- get protection from the other spouse's debts, and
- reach other financial agreements, such as how you will buy a house together, start a business, put each other through college, or set aside money for savings.

While state laws vary, in general, you cannot use a prenup to restrict child support, custody, or visitation rights, encourage divorce (by appearing to offer a financial incentive for one spouse to end the marriage), or make rules about nonfinancial matters, such as having and raising children, or how you'll share household chores. In a few states, you can't use a prenup to give up the right to alimony.

Lawyers and Prenups

To get started, an engaged couple should evaluate their circumstances, agree on what they want their prenuptial agreement to cover, and even start writing a draft of it. Most states require (or least suggest) that each person have an independent lawyer review the agreement, and it's a good idea whether your state requires it or not. Having two independent lawyers involved will help you craft a lasting agreement that both of you understand, and will help avoid court fights should you end up in an acrimonious divorce. In particular, if one spouse has much less money or assets than the other, the lower-earning spouse must have an attorney; otherwise, if there's ever a lawsuit over the prenup, the court may set it aside because the weaker party didn't have good advice.

If you make a prenup, be sure to follow through by making your estate plan. For example, if you are using a prenup to waive inheritance rights, make sure that your will and other estate planning documents actually transfer property as you intend. The prenup itself isn't enough to make sure your wishes are carried out.

RESOURCE

Help with prenuptial agreements. Before you visit a lawyer, you can decide essential terms and begin drafting your own prenuptial agreement, using Nolo's *Prenuptial Agreements: How to Write a Fair & Lasting Contract*, by Katherine E. Stoner and Shae Irving. This book includes a summary of each state's prenuptial laws. See www.nolo.com for a sample chapter and full table of contents.

Green Cards for Fiancés or Spouses

If you are a U.S. citizen or permanent resident, and you are engaged or married to a citizen of another country, your fiancé or spouse may be eligible for a green card. This includes a same-sex marriage, if legally valid in the state or country where it took place.

However, many people believe, wrongly, that they can just bring their fiancé or spouse to the United States or (if the immigrant is already here) to an office of U.S. Citizenship and Immigration Services (USCIS) and the immigrant will be given an instant green card or even U.S. citizenship—a belief that has led to sad cases of people being sent right home again.

The reality is that your fiancé or spouse will have to go through a multistep application process. It's your job to start the process, by submitting to USCIS either a fiancé visa petition (Form I-129F) or an immigrant visa petition (Form I-130).

A fiancé or spouse who is currently overseas won't be allowed to enter the United States until both the visa petition and subsequent applications have been approved.

If your fiancé or spouse is already in the United States, the process gets even more complicated. A very recent entry by the immigrant on a tourist visa with the intention of applying for a green card could be considered visa fraud and disqualify your spouse for a green card. Completing the application process at a USCIS office within the United States is not permitted for some immigrants, depending on whether you (the petitioning spouse) are a U.S. citizen and whether your immigrant spouse entered the United States lawfully. That leads to further problems, because if your spouse has no choice but to leave the United States to complete the application process, but has lived in the United States illegally, your spouse may face a penalty and be forced to spend years outside the United States before returning.

(Fortunately, there's a waiver certain categories of immigrants can apply for before leaving the U.S., called a "provisional waiver.")

Even if everything goes right, be prepared for a long wait. Every type of visa application involves several stages, including application forms, a medical examination, fingerprinting, various approvals, and an interview with a U.S. government official.

> ! CAUTION
>
> **If you're not yet a U.S. citizen.** If you have U.S. permanent residence (a green card), you cannot bring your fiancé to the United States until you're married. Even then, your spouse will have to spend some years on a waiting list before entering the country. Work on getting U.S. citizenship to speed things up.

Eligibility for Fiancé and Marriage Visas

The basic requirements for the fiancé visa and the marriage visa are different.

Fiancé Visas

To qualify for a fiancé visa, the immigrant must intend to marry a U.S. citizen (same or opposite sex), have met the citizen in person within the last two years, and be legally able to marry under the laws of the state where the wedding will be held.

Also, the immigrant must be living in another country— someone who is already in the United States isn't eligible for a fiancé visa.

As part of the fiancé visa application process, you'll have to prove your intention to marry. That means providing a selection of documents, such as copies of your love letters, wedding announcement, emails, and wedding ceremony contracts for services such as catering and flowers. You'll also have to prove that you've met within the last two years, by submitting copies of plane tickets, hotel bills, or any other relevant documents.

Marriage-Based Visas (Green Cards)

To be eligible for an immigrant visa or a green card based on marriage, the immigrant must be legally married (it doesn't matter in what country) to a U.S. citizen or permanent resident (same or opposite sex). Neither the immigrant nor the U.S. spouse can be married to someone else.

In the application process, you'll have to prove all of these things. Legal marriage is usually the easiest to prove, simply by providing a copy of your marriage certificate. Do your best to get your marriage certificate from a government office. Unless it's all that's available in the country where you were married, USCIS will reject a certificate from a ship's captain, church, or another nongovernmental place.

A binational marriage must be the real thing, not just a sham to get a green card. You'll have to prove that your marriage is for real by providing copies of documents such as joint bank statements, children's birth certificates, photos of the wedding and honeymoon, correspondence that demonstrates an intimate relationship, and more. Also, near the end of the application process, you'll have to attend an interview, either at an overseas

U.S. consulate or (in the rare case where the immigrant is in the United States and eligible to complete the green card application process here) at a USCIS office. Similar to what you've seen in the movies, an interviewing officer who suspects fraud may separate you and your spouse and ask you detailed personal questions about your marriage and your life together.

Inadmissibility

To qualify for any type of visa, an immigrant must show that he or she is not "inadmissible." A person who can't show a means of support in the United States outside of public assistance, who has a criminal record or associations with a terrorist organization, who has committed visa fraud or repeatedly entered the United States illegally and been removed, who has spent more than six months in the U.S. unlawfully, or who abuses drugs or has a communicable disease like tuberculosis would not be admitted to the United States. Inadmissibility is a major stumbling block for many immigrants, though waivers are available in some cases.

What's Next in the Green Card Application Process?

How and where an immigrant actually applies for a green card depends on a number of factors. These can include the immigration status of the person the immigrant is marrying, whether or not the immigrant is in the United States already, and, if so, whether the person got here legally. In some cases, particularly where inadmissibility may be an issue, hiring an experienced immigration attorney is well worth the cost.

RESOURCE

More on fiancé and marriage visas:

The Immigration section of www.nolo.com includes many useful articles on U.S. green cards, visas, and citizenship, including eligibility and sponsorship requirements, interviews, exams, and bringing your fiancé or spouse to the United States.

Fiancé & Marriage Visas: A Couple's Guide to U.S. Immigration, by Ilona Bray (Nolo), can help you complete the application forms, assemble the appropriate documents, and have a successful interview. See www.nolo.com for a sample chapter and full table of contents.

Same-Sex Marriage

In the last two decades, the legal landscape for same-sex couples has changed in extraordinary ways and continues to evolve rapidly. Legal marriage is now available to any same-sex couple willing to travel to a marriage equality state—although the marriage will now be recognized by the federal government, it may not be recognized by the couple's home state if they reside in a nonrecognition jurisdiction. In short, for same-sex couples, marriage is a lot more complicated than just saying "I do."

States That Allow Same-Sex Marriages

As of the time of this writing, 19 states and the District of Columbia allow a same-sex couple to get married and enjoy all of the benefits of marriage under their laws.

States Where Same-Sex Couples Can Marry		
California	Maine	New York
Connecticut	Maryland	Oregon
Delaware	Massachusetts	Pennsylvania
District of Columbia	Minnesota	Rhode Island
Hawaii	New Hampshire	Vermont
Illinois	New Jersey	Washington
Iowa	New Mexico	

While these marriages are legal for all purposes in the state where they are entered into, and the federal government now recognizes same-sex marriages, many states refuse such recognition (see "Federal Nonrecognition Issues," below).

All of the states that allow same-sex marriage recognize same-sex marriages—as well as civil unions and domestic partnerships—performed elsewhere. In these states, as long as you were legally married in a state or country that allows same-sex marriage, you will be treated like any other married couple: You can file a joint state tax return, provide health and retirement benefits for your spouse if you work for the state government, and enjoy numerous other rights that come with marriage under state laws, including divorce, child custody, property division, family leave benefits, and medical rights such as hospital visitation.

Federal Nonrecognition Issues

On a federal level, recognition issues changed dramatically in 2013, when the United States Supreme Court issued a historic decision in *United States v. Windsor*. The Court struck down the federal definition of marriage under the federal Defense of Marriage Act or "DOMA," which limited marriage to a union between a man and a woman.

The DOMA case involved Edith Windsor and Thea Spyer, a lesbian couple that was married in Canada in 2007—after being in a relationship for 40 years. When Spyer died in 2009, Windsor was forced to pay $363,053 in federal taxes on Spyer's estate, which she would not have had to pay if she'd been Spyer's husband. She argued that DOMA, which prevented her from being considered Spyer's spouse for federal purposes, cost her $363,053.

In a 5–4 decision, the Court found that the section of DOMA defining marriage as between a man and a woman violates the Equal Protection Clause and is therefore unconstitutional.

Now, under *Windsor*, legally married same-sex couples are considered "married" in the federal government's eyes and eligible for federal benefits in the same way that opposite-sex married couples are. However, the eligibility rules vary among federal agencies and as a result, some same-sex married couples living in nonrecognition states will not qualify for all federal benefits.

The Place of Celebration Rule

Many federal agencies, such as the U.S. Citizenship and Immigration Services (USCIS) and the U.S. Office of

Personnel & Management look to the "place of celebration" (where the marriage was performed) to determine whether same-sex married couples are eligible for benefits. Under this rule, if you're in a valid marriage, you will qualify for federal benefits even if you live in a nonrecognition state.

The same goes for the IRS and eligibility for federal tax benefits. In August 2013, the U.S. Department of Treasury issued a ruling, which states all same-sex couples that are legally married in any U.S. state, the District of Columbia, a U.S. territory, or a foreign country will be recognized as married under all federal tax provisions where marriage is a factor.

The Treasury Department further clarified that federal recognition for tax purposes applies whether a same-sex married couple lives in a jurisdiction that recognizes same-sex marriage (such as California) or a nonrecognition jurisdiction (such as Texas). But the decision does not apply to same-sex couples in domestic partnerships or civil unions.

The Place of Domicile Rule

Some federal agencies, such as the Social Security Administration, only recognize marriages that are valid in the "place of domicile" (where the couple lives) for the purposes of granting federal benefits. This means if you're in a same-sex marriage, but live in a nonrecognition state, you aren't eligible for Social Security benefits on your spouse's work record. If you live in one of the 20 jurisdictions that recognize same-sex marriage (listed in the chart above), you will qualify for benefits. This also applies to Medicaid and Supplemental Security Income, Medicare, bankruptcy filings, and benefits under the Family Medical Leave Act. These rules may change in the future, but this is where things stand now.

If you are in a domestic partnership or civil union in any of the states that offer those relationship options, none of the benefits of marriage under federal law will apply to you because the federal government doesn't yet recognize these same-sex relationships.

State Nonrecognition Issues

On a state level, nonrecognition means that a couple can travel to a marriage-equality state, get legally married, and then return home to their nonrecognition state and find that their marriage has very little meaning where they live. In at least two states, judges have refused to grant divorces to married same-sex couples because the state where the couple sought the divorce did not recognize the marriage itself. This leaves the couple in the position of having to either stay married or move to a state where the marriage is recognized and establish residency (which can take as long as six months to a year) in order to file for divorce there.

Domestic Partnerships and Civil Unions

A number of states have established legal relationships that are the functional equivalent of marriage for same-sex couples but are called something else—either domestic partnerships or civil unions. The term "domestic partners" is somewhat confusing, because it is used to describe legal marriage equivalent relationships; legal relationships that only provide partial marital rights; and unmarried couples, of the same or opposite sex, who live together in a family relationship, and in some cases are recognized by local governments, businesses, colleges, and universities.

Marriage Equivalent Relationships

California, Nevada, Oregon, Washington State, and the District of Columbia offer domestic partnership status that is the functional equivalent of marriage; Colorado, Hawaii, and Illinois do the same but call the relationship a civil union. (Now that same-sex marriage is legal in Illinois and Hawaii, it remains unclear whether these states will continue to grant and recognize civil unions or convert civil unions into marriages at a later date.) Some of these states limit domestic partnership registration to same-sex couples, but some include opposite-sex couples in which one partner is 62 or older. (This is to avoid affecting Social Security benefits, which can sometimes be reduced when the person receiving benefits gets married.)

No license is required to enter a domestic partnership or civil union—usually it's just a matter of filing a notarized form with a state office like the secretary of state. Ending a domestic partnership or civil union in a marriage equivalent state usually requires that the partners go through the same court procedures that opposite-sex couples must use. There may be an abbreviated process for couples who haven't been registered for very long and don't own any property, but not many people qualify for that. Couples living in a non-recognition state generally need some legal advice on how to terminate their domestic partnership or civil union. (Chapter 2, "Divorce," provides more detail on ending a same-sex marriage or domestic partnership.)

Limited Rights and Benefits

Wisconsin provides for some form of legal relationship, but the rights that come along with its domestic partnership are a far cry from the marital rights provided in the marriage-equality and marriage equivalent states.

In addition to these state level rights and benefits, some public and private entities may offer domestic partners benefits such as health, dental, and vision insurance, sick and bereavement leave, accident and life insurance, death benefits, parental leave (for a child you coparent), housing rights and tuition reduction (at universities), and use of recreational facilities.

RESOURCE

Helpful resources on same-sex marriage, domestic partnerships, and civil unions:

For details on laws in your state, including municipalities and other entities offering domestic partnership benefits, see the "Marriage Updates" section of www.lambdalegal.org, or call 866-542-8336. Also, see the National Center for Lesbian Rights (www.nclrights.org, phone 800-528-6257), a national lesbian and gay legal organization that provides education, resources, and support.

Making It Legal: A Guide to Same-Sex Marriage, Domestic Partnerships & Civil Unions, by Frederick Hertz with Emily Doskow, fully explains same-sex relationship laws, reviews key issues that influence the decision to marry, and offers practical guidance. You can see a sample chapter and the full table of contents at www.nolo.com.

The LGBT Law section of www.nolo.com contains a wide range of articles that discuss issues affecting gay and lesbian couples.

Common Law Marriage

In many states, heterosexual couples can become legally married without a license or ceremony. This type of marriage is called a common law marriage. Contrary to popular belief, a common law marriage is not created when two people simply live together for a certain number of years. To have a valid common law marriage (in states that recognize it), the couple must do all of the following:

- live together for a significant period of time (not defined in any state)
- hold themselves out as a married couple—typically this means using the same last name, referring to the other as "my husband" or "my wife," and filing a joint tax return, and
- intend to be married.

Common law marriages are not that common—they're actually fairly unusual. When one exists, the spouses receive the same legal treatment given to formally married couples, including the requirement that they go through a legal divorce to end the marriage.

Living Together

Many laws control the property ownership rights of married couples. In most states, no such laws exist for the many unmarried couples who live together, except for the handful of states with marriage-like domestic partnerships or civil unions. If you and your partner (gay or straight) are unmarried, you must take steps to protect your relationship and define your property rights. You will also face special concerns if you are raising children together.

Preparing a Written Property Agreement

If you want to legally establish how you will own property during your relationship, as well as what will happen if you separate or if one of you dies, you must put your intentions, desires, and expectations in writing. Your agreement will be called a "nonmarital agreement" or "living together contract." (Or, if you are planning for what happens when you die, you'll need to make a will.)

Almost all states now enforce written contracts between unmarried partners. And the longer you live together, the more important it is to write a contract making it clear who owns what. Otherwise, you might face a serious (and potentially expensive) battle if you split up and can't agree on how to divide what you've acquired.

A written property agreement is particularly important if you buy a house together. It should cover all of the following:

- **How you will take title to the property.** Your options vary from state to state. Many states let you hold title as "joint tenants with rights of survivorship," meaning that when one partner dies, the other automatically inherits the whole house. Or you might want to hold title as "tenants in common," so that each owner can choose who gets that partner's share by making a will or trust.

- **How much of the house each partner owns.** If you're joint tenants, then in most states, you must own equal shares.
- **What happens to the house if you break up.** Will one of you buy out the other, or will you sell the house and divide the proceeds? If you don't agree on who can buy the other out, how will you decide who gets first choice?

Inheriting From an Unmarried Partner

If your unmarried partner dies, will you inherit? Not automatically. Your rights depend on whether your late partner made a will, trust, joint tenancy agreement, or some other estate planning document to leave property to you.

Making Medical Decisions for an Unmarried Partner

If you are injured or incapacitated, your partner will not be allowed to make medical or financial decisions on your behalf unless you have executed the appropriate documents. To give your partner the right to make medical decisions for you, you must sign a form called a "durable power of attorney" (sometimes included in a "health care directive"). Without a durable power of attorney, the fate of a severely ill or injured person could be in the hands of a biological relative who won't honor the wishes of the ill or injured person. It is far better to prepare the necessary paperwork so the loving and knowing partner will be the decision maker. If you want your partner to be able to make financial decisions for you—when you become incapacitated or even for a short time because you're out of the country or otherwise unavailable—you need to execute another type of power of attorney, one that covers financial matters.

Paternity, Custody, and Adoption

Unmarried same-sex couples who have children together need to take special steps when it comes to children. Unmarried heterosexual couples, on the other hand, aren't generally treated any differently than married straight couples from a legal perspective. Later chapters explain how you can head off problems over custody (covered in Chapter 3) and adoption (see Chapter 5).

Changing Your Name

Some unmarried couples want to share a last name. If you don't have a marriage certificate, you will need a court order (this is usually fairly simple) to change your name. For more information, see www.nolo.com/legal-encyclopedia/name-change.

Handling Housing Discrimination

In most states, landlords may legally refuse to rent to an unmarried couple. About 20 states ban discrimination on the basis of marital status, and most of them protect married couples only. Federal law does not protect unmarried couples from housing discrimination. Housing discrimination based on sexual orientation and gender identity, however, is prohibited in many states and cities. Many of these laws also protect unmarried heterosexual couples.

Check your state fair housing agency for laws that apply to you. To find your state information, see the U.S. Department of Housing and Urban Development (HUD) website at portal. hud.gov/hudportal/HUD/states.

RESOURCE

For unmarried couples:

Living Together: A Legal Guide for Unmarried Couples, by Ralph Warner, Toni Ihara, and Frederick Hertz (Nolo), explains the legal rules that apply to unmarried couples and includes sample contracts about jointly owned property. See www.nolo.com for a sample chapter and full table of contents.

A Legal Guide for Lesbian & Gay Couples, by Frederick Hertz and Emily Doskow (Nolo), sets out the law on everything from medical and financial issues to parenting and estate planning and contains useful sample agreements. See www.nolo.com for a sample chapter and full table of contents.

Wills and Estate Planning for Families

Writing a will should be at the top of your estate planning list, especially if you have children. (If you're married, each spouse makes a separate will.) With a will you can:

Determine who gets what after your death. Generally, the largest part of people's estates goes to a spouse, long-term partner, or children. Only property you own entirely yourself and that you have not already named a beneficiary for will pass through your will. A house owned in joint tenancy or a retirement account for which you've named a beneficiary, for example, will not pass through your will.

Name an executor, the person who has a legal responsibility to carry out the terms of your will and handle your property after your death. The person you choose as executor should be trustworthy, conscientious, and good at keeping track of details. Most people name a spouse, close friend, or relative as executor.

Choose a personal guardian for your children, someone who will raise your children in the unlikely event that you and the other parent can't. You should have complete confidence in the person you nominate and you should be certain that this person is willing to accept this big responsibility should the need arise. A guardian's legal authority comes from a court. So if a guardian were ever needed for your children, a probate judge would look at your will and appoint your nominee, unless the judge concluded that it was not in the best interests of your children to so do.

Name a property manager, someone to manage money children inherit until the children are old enough to manage it.

Choose someone who is a good money manager, responsible, trustworthy, and diligent. Ideally, this will be the same person you name as your child's personal guardian, but it doesn't need to be. There are various ways you can use your will to give the person you've chosen control over a child's money, including setting up a trust for each child.

A Spouse's Right to Inherit

If you're married and live in one of the nine community property states (listed above), you and your spouse each automatically own half of all the property and earnings (with a few exceptions) each of you acquires during your marriage. So each of you can leave your half of the community property, and all of your separate property (generally all property you owned before marriage or received through gift or inheritance), to anyone you choose.

In all other states (common law property states, also discussed above), there is no rule that property acquired during marriage is owned by both spouses. Property generally belongs to the spouse who earns it or whose name is on the title document. To protect spouses from being disinherited, common law property states give a surviving spouse a legal right to claim a portion of the deceased spouse's estate, even if the will says something different.

These rules also apply to registered domestic partners and couples in civil unions in states that offer these options.

Generally, it's legal to disinherit a child.

RESOURCE

Estate planning resources from Nolo. *Quicken WillMaker Plus* software lets you create a valid will, customized to the laws in your state, and many other important estate planning documents. For information on *WillMaker* and other Nolo estate planning titles, including books for executors and people in second marriages, see the Wills, Trusts, & Probate section of www.nolo.com.

For information on other estate planning documents, see "Health Care Directives and Power of Attorney Forms" In Chapter 7.

Divorce

Divorce is the legal termination of a marriage. Couples separate, divide their property (everything from the house to the retirement accounts), and, if necessary, make arrangements for child custody and support.

Although states use different rules for dividing property and dealing with children of a marriage, the basic procedures of divorce follow the same general pattern everywhere. The process is always both paperwork-heavy and emotionally challenging, but couples can now take advantage of increasingly available services like mediation and collaborative divorce. Those who do usually end up feeling less damaged by the process than those who are determined to fight everything out in court. And many lawyers are choosing to embrace a less adversarial model, encouraging divorcing couples to resolve financial and family issues as amicably as possible.

 STATE RULES

State divorce rules. The Divorce, Child Support & Child Custody section of Nolo's website (www.nolo.com/legal-encyclopedia/child-support) contains state rules on grounds for divorce, residency requirements, how property is divided, and resources for do-it-yourself divorce.

Separation or Divorce

Separation simply means that you are living apart from your spouse. You're still legally married until you get a judgment of divorce from a court. There are three kinds of separation: trial, permanent, and legal. In most states, all three have the potential to affect your legal rights regarding property ownership.

Trial Separation

You and your spouse may choose to live apart for a trial period while you decide between divorce or reconciliation. Your living arrangements don't change the legal rules that control the ownership of property. For example, if you live in a community property state, money you earn still belongs equally to you and your spouse. And if you are in a common law state, a debt you incur on your own probably isn't your spouse's responsibility.

If you and your spouse are hoping to reconcile, it's a good idea to write an informal agreement about some issues that will surely come up while you are separated. For example, will you continue to share a joint bank account? Who will stay in the family home? If you have young children, how and when will each of you spend time with them?

If you decide there's no going back, your trial separation turns into a permanent one.

Permanent Separation

When you live apart from your spouse without intending to reconcile, but you are not divorced, you are considered permanently separated. In most states, this type of separation can change property rights between spouses: If you don't intend to get back together, then assets and debts acquired during the separation belong only to the spouse who acquires them. Once you are permanently separated, you are no longer responsible for any debts that your spouse incurs. Similarly, you're no longer entitled to any share of property or income that your spouse acquires or earns.

Legal Separation

In some (not all) states, you can get a legal separation by filing a request in court. People choose legal separation instead of divorce because of religious beliefs, a desire to keep the family together legally for the sake of children, the need for one spouse to keep the health insurance benefits that would be lost with a divorce, or simple aversion to divorcing despite the desire to live separate lives.

If you're legally separated, you're no longer married, but you're not divorced either, and you can't remarry. The court's order granting the legal separation includes orders about property division, alimony, and child custody and support, just as a divorce would. In states where legal separation isn't allowed, you have to choose either divorce or an informal separation with agreements between you and your spouse about how you deal with your marital property.

Domestic Violence

If you're in danger of physical abuse at home, get out and get help as soon as you possibly can. Many communities have women's shelters where women and children who are victims of domestic violence can stay until the crisis passes or until they find a permanent home. To find shelters and related services, consult the local police, welfare department, neighborhood resource center, or women's center. You may also want to get a temporary restraining order (TRO) from a court. A TRO orders the violent partner to leave you alone. It may require, for example, that the perpetrator stay away from the family home, your workplace or school, your children's school, and other places you frequent, such as a gym, friend's house, or church.

Useful resources include:

- National Coalition Against Domestic Violence (NCADV), 303-839-1852, www.ncadv.org. Provides information and resources, including links to relevant state agencies.
- National Domestic Violence Hotline, 800-799-SAFE (7233), www.thehotline.org. Provides information to callers—gay or straight.
- WomensLaw.org, www.womenslaw.org. Provides state-by-state information and resources on domestic violence.

Annulment

Like a divorce, an annulment granted by a court ends a marriage. But, unlike a divorce, when you get an annulment, it's as though you were never married, at least in some ways. Although you need to divide your property just like other divorcing couples, you are legally entitled to call yourself "single" after the annulment.

Religion is the most common reason for choosing annulment over divorce. In particular, the Roman Catholic Church doesn't sanction divorce or subsequent remarriage, but does allow someone whose first marriage was annulled by the Church to remarry in the Church. But even if you get a religious annulment, in order to end your marital relationship in the eyes of the state, you must obtain a civil annulment through the courts.

Although most annulments take place very soon after the wedding, some couples seek annulments after they have been married for many years. In that case, the court considers all of the same issues as in a divorce: Property is divided, and support and custody decisions are made. Children of a marriage that has been annulled are still legally considered "legitimate" children of the marriage.

In most places, you can get a civil annulment for one of the following reasons: fraud or misrepresentation; no consummation of the marriage; incest, bigamy, or underage party; unsound mind (one or both of the spouses was impaired by alcohol or drugs at the time of the wedding or didn't have the mental capacity to understand what was happening); or force (one of the parties was forced into getting married).

Divorce and Family Court Proceedings

Every divorce case goes through some sort of court proceeding. Even if you and your spouse agree about how you will divide your property and handle custody, visitation, and support issues, a judge must still grant your divorce (or dissolution, as it's called in some places).

In most states, divorce cases—whether contested or not— are handled by a special court or a specific department, called "family court," "domestic relations court," or "divorce court." Most states have fill-in-the-blanks forms for divorce cases, available from the local courthouse or court.

Where Can You Get Divorced? State Residency Requirements

Nearly all states require a spouse to be a resident of the state for a certain length of time, commonly six weeks to one year, before filing for a divorce there. If you file for divorce, you must show proof of having lived in the state for the required length of time.

If one spouse meets a state residency requirement, a divorce obtained in that state is valid even if the other spouse lives somewhere else, as long as there was jurisdiction over the non-resident spouse. The court gets jurisdiction if the nonresident spouse is personally given (served with) the divorce documents; consents to jurisdiction by showing up at a court date or signing an affidavit of service, acknowledging receipt of the filed legal documents; or abides by the court's rulings—for example, by paying court-ordered child support.

If jurisdiction was proper, the courts of all states will recognize the divorce and any decisions the court makes regarding property division, alimony, custody, and child support.

Kinds of Divorce

There's not just one way to divorce. Most states offer different paths, depending largely on whether or not you and your spouse can agree on financial and custody matters or need a judge to decide these issues for you. There are also legal differences; some states allow you to prove fault, and some don't.

Check your local superior or family court website for information on the procedure you'll need to follow and the paperwork you'll need to submit.

Summary Divorce

In many states, an expedited divorce procedure is available to a minority of couples who haven't been married for very long (usually five years or less), don't own much property, don't have children, and don't have significant joint debts. Both spouses need to agree to the divorce, and you must file court papers jointly.

A summary (sometimes called simplified) divorce involves a lot less paperwork than other types of divorce—a few forms are often all it takes. You can probably get the forms you need from the local family court. For this reason, summary divorces are usually easy to do yourself, without the help of a lawyer.

Uncontested Divorce

In an uncontested divorce, you and your spouse work together to agree on the terms of your divorce and file court papers cooperatively to make the divorce happen. There will be no formal trial, and you probably won't have to ever appear in court. Instead, you file court forms, such as a petition, and a "marital settlement agreement" (MSA) that details your agreements about how you want to divide property and debts and any support payments. Custody arrangements for your children will either be in the MSA or in a parenting agreement that's attached to your MSA or stands alone as a separate agreement. Your settlement, and your final divorce, will have to be approved by a judge. That shouldn't be any problem unless it's clear that the terms are completely unfair to one spouse or that one person was under duress.

Many courts provide plain-English information and simplified forms to make it relatively easy to handle an uncontested divorce without a lawyer. But you may want to ask a lawyer to look over your paperwork and, perhaps, to help draft or review your settlement agreement. Some other experts who might be useful include: a counselor or a mediator to help you come to agreement on property and custody issues;

an accountant to help you figure out the tax consequences of spousal support or property division; a lawyer to prepare the special court order (called a Qualified Domestic Relations Order, or QDRO) you'll need to divide retirement benefits; an appraiser to determine the market value of your house; or an accountant or actuary to help value an investment like a small business or a pension.

If you and your spouse both stay on top of all the tasks you need to take care of, you should be able to finalize your divorce as soon as the waiting period (every state has one) is over. (Waiting periods generally range from three to six months.)

Default Divorce

The court will grant a divorce by "default" if you file for divorce and your spouse doesn't respond. The divorce is granted even though your spouse doesn't participate in the court proceedings at all. A default divorce might happen, for example, if your spouse has left for parts unknown and can't be found.

Fault and No-Fault Divorce

"No-fault" describes any divorce where the spouse suing for divorce does not have to prove that the other spouse did something wrong. Every state offers the option of no-fault divorce—and in many states, no-fault is the only option.

In a classic no-fault divorce, instead of proving that one spouse is to blame, you merely tell the court that you and your spouse have "irreconcilable differences" or have suffered an "irremediable breakdown" of your relationship or give some other reason recognized by the state. In some states, you must also have lived apart for a specified period of time.

In some states, you have a choice of using fault or no-fault grounds for divorce. Traditional grounds in a fault divorce are cruelty (inflicting unnecessary emotional or physical pain), adultery, or desertion. Some people choose a fault divorce because they don't want to wait out the period of separation required by their state's laws for a no-fault divorce. And in some states, a spouse who proves the other's fault may receive a greater share of the marital property or more alimony or get custody of the children. Even if you choose no-fault, some state courts still use fault as a factor in a no-fault divorce, when setting alimony, dividing property, or deciding custody—for example, a spouse who has deserted the family might receive a lesser share of the assets.

Mediated Divorce

In a mediation, you and your spouse jointly hire a trained, neutral third party, called a mediator—often a lawyer—to help you negotiate and reach a settlement. Mediation is often used in divorce cases to work out financial issues and property division, and some jurisdictions may require parents to work with a court-appointed mediator to try and work out a mutually agreeable custody or visitation schedule before the judge will hear the case. (Chapter 3 discusses mediation in child custody cases.) A divorcing couple may also work with a private mediator to negotiate financial disputes over property and support (spousal and child). When you reach an agreement with an opposing party through mediation, you can make it legally binding by writing down your decisions in the form of an enforceable contract. The attorneys for one or both parties will usually finalize and approve the agreement. You may also want to consult with a lawyer before starting mediation to discuss the legal consequences of possible settlement terms.

Mediating instead of litigating will nearly always be less costly (and quicker) than fighting over an issue in court will, and minimize negative effects on children. Mediation sessions are usually scheduled quickly, and most sessions last only a few hours or a day, depending on the type of case. In contrast, lawsuits often take many months, or even years, to resolve. Private divorce mediation, where a couple aims to settle all the issues in their divorce—property division and alimony, as well as child custody, visitation, and support—may require half a dozen or more mediation sessions spread over several weeks or months.

Another advantage of mediation is confidentiality. With very few exceptions (for example, where a criminal act or child abuse is involved), what you say during mediation cannot legally be revealed outside the mediation proceedings or used later in a court of law.

Will Divorce Mediation Work for You?

You are most likely to have a successful mediation if all or most of the following statements are true:

- The decision to divorce is mutual.
- You have no desire to reconcile.
- You want to stay on good terms with your spouse.
- You understand the financial reality with which you are working.
- Your spouse has not lied to you about anything important.
- You are not easily intimidated by your spouse.
- Physical violence, alcohol, or drug abuse are not issues in your relationship.
- You feel that your spouse is a good parent—and you want to work out a custody arrangement that is in the best interests of your child.

RESOURCE

Private divorce mediations are usually handled by sole practitioners or small, local mediation groups. A good online source of information is www.mediate.com, 541-345-1629. Before choosing a mediator, get referrals and interview them like you would a lawyer.

Collaborative Divorce

In a collaborative divorce, you and your spouse each hire a lawyer—but not just any lawyer. You want ones who have been trained to work cooperatively and who agree to try to settle your case without going to court—and if you aren't able to do that, the lawyers agree to bow out and you must hire new lawyers for the court proceeding. So, although each of you has a lawyer who is on your side, much of the work is done in cooperation. Each of you agrees to disclose all the information that's necessary for fair negotiations and to meet with each other and both lawyers to discuss settlement. Often other professionals—usually an accountant, actuary, and a therapist—are involved in the process.

Contested Divorce

If you and your spouse argue so much over property or child custody that you can't come to an agreement and, instead, take these issues to the judge, you have what's called a contested divorce. The judge, court clerks, and the attorneys (yours and your spouse's) will be the main players in your divorce case.

A divorce trial itself may be short (just a day or so), but the process is hard, painful, and likely to take years. In addition to the huge emotional toll on you and your family, a contested divorce, even one that ends in a settlement rather than a trial, can cost each spouse many tens of thousands of dollars.

Will You Need a Lawyer?

If your divorce is simple and uncontested, you might decide to do it yourself and not hire a lawyer at all. Or, you can use a lawyer as a mediator or a collaborative representative or to handle only specific parts of your divorce. For example, a consulting lawyer can explain your rights and the legal procedures you're dealing with, provide referrals to other professionals like actuaries or appraisers, or give you advice about one particular aspect of your divorce (such as alimony or custody) or documents (such as your marital settlement agreement).

On the other hand, if you can't work out issues involving children, property, and money with your spouse, especially if your spouse is being dishonest or vindictive, you will want to hire your own attorney. You'll definitely want to do so if there is a problem with abuse (spousal, child, sexual, or substance). A lawyer can help you get the arrangement you need to protect yourself and your children, such as getting a temporary order to keep your spouse away or for custody of your children, or filing a request in court for child support.

Even if you have a fairly good relationship with your ex, you may want to hire your own lawyer if a lot of property and assets are involved in your divorce—particularly if you have not been the main breadwinner or if you have a prenuptial agreement. For example, you may be especially concerned that you get your fair share of retirement accounts or that your spouse could be hiding assets.

Divorce for Same-Sex Couples

Numerous states offer some form of relationship recognition for same-sex couples, each state having different rules—and, of course, the rules are changing rapidly. In addition, some cities and counties offer local registration, with varying benefits. (See Chapter 1 for details.) And the only things more confusing than the mishmash of rules for forming same-sex marriages, civil unions, and domestic partnerships are the rules for ending those relationships.

Terminating a Marriage, State Domestic Partnership, or Civil Union

To terminate a legal same-sex marriage or marriage-equivalent state registration, you must go through the same divorce process in court that opposite-sex married couples do. If you don't legally end the relationship, your legal obligations, which are generally the same as those of married couples, will continue. For example, you could be on the hook for your ex-partner's credit card debts, could be ordered to share some of your savings with your ex, and could find yourself paying spousal support. Just as is true for opposite-sex married couples, there is a streamlined procedure for same-sex couples who haven't been together long and don't have kids or own property, but most people don't qualify.

Terminating a state registration or marriage can be complicated. If you live in a state that doesn't recognize same-sex relationships and you went elsewhere to marry or register, the local court may refuse to grant a divorce. If you have multiple registrations from different states, the judge may be even more reluctant to end all of them. You may need to go back to the state where you registered or married and complete the process there—but most states have residency requirements, some as long as a year.

Because this area of law is confusing and changing quickly, you're best off finding a local divorce lawyer experienced in same-sex divorces to help you through the process.

RESOURCE

Attorneys experienced in same-sex divorces. Contact the National Center for Lesbian Rights at www.nclrights.org or call 800-528-6257 for information and referrals.

Terminating a Local Partnership Registration

If you and a partner registered with the city or county, or with your employer, you don't need to go to court to terminate that relationship. You should still end the registration, but if you don't, you're not likely to run into a lot of financial consequences. Local registrations are easy to end, as are registrations with your employer that you entered for insurance purposes. Each city, county, and business has a termination form, and you simply have to get it, fill it out, and send it in.

Property, Custody, and Support

Every divorcing couple must consider how property and debts will be divided and whether one spouse will pay spousal support to the other. If you have minor children, you'll also need to make decisions about support and parenting time. You and your spouse will either need to work out these three big issues or, if you just can't do it, turn them over to a judge to decide. Even if you work out your agreements, the judge will have to approve them.

Dividing Assets and Property

"Marital property" is the collection of assets you and your spouse have earned or acquired during your marriage, including your savings, house, investments, cars, pension plans, and the like. Marital debts are obligations you took on together during your married life.

In general, both the property and the debts belong to both of you, and part of the divorce process will be to divide them up between you. If you prepared a prenuptial agreement, some of these decisions may have already been made. And assets or debts that either of you had before your marriage, or that you acquired after the permanent separation, are called separate property or debts. Some property that one spouse acquired during marriage (such as a car bought with separate income with title held in one spouse's name alone) may also be separate property, depending on state law. Generally, when you divorce, each of you will keep your separate property and be responsible for your separate debts, but, in some states, separate property can be divided at divorce.

Who Stays in the House

If children are involved, the parent who provides their primary care usually remains in the marital home with them. If you don't have children and the house is the separate property of just one spouse, that spouse has the legal right to ask the other to leave. If, however, you own the house together, this question gets tricky, particularly if you have children and share equally in their care. Neither of you has a greater legal right than the other to stay in the house. If you and your spouse don't come to a decision, the court will decide for you during divorce proceedings. Or, if you need a quick decision, you can ask for a temporary court order on the issue. That will require a short hearing before a judge. Temporary orders are usually valid until the court holds another hearing or the spouses arrive at their own settlement through negotiation or mediation.

If you and your spouse can agree on how to divide your assets and property, the court will simply approve your agreement. The terms will go into a court judgment or a document called a marital settlement agreement.

If you can't agree, the court will divide things for you. The nine community property states (listed in Chapter 1) divide marital property equally. The rest (known as common law property states) use a system of "equitable distribution," to divide property in a way that the court thinks is fair, but that isn't always equal. For example, two-thirds of the assets may go to the lower wage earner and one-third to the other spouse.

Working Out Child Custody and Support Arrangements

You and your spouse (or the court if you can't reach agreement) will need to decide whether you'll share custody of your children equally, or whether one parent will be the primary custodial parent. Custody means both the right to have a child live with you (physical custody) and the right to make decisions about the child's welfare and education (legal custody). (Chapter 3 covers these issues in detail.)

Chances are that one parent will pay child support to the other, to make sure that the kids are always taken care of. Each state has guidelines for calculating child support, based on the amount of time each parent spends with the children and the amount each parent earns, as well as factors such as who pays for the children's health insurance or child care. (Chapter 4 addresses child support.)

Alimony

In some divorces, courts award alimony, also called spousal support, to one party. A support award is especially likely after a long marriage or if one spouse gave up career plans to support the other spouse or care for kids.

How Alimony Amount and Duration Are Determined

Divorcing spouses can agree on the amount and length of time alimony will be paid. But if you can't agree, a court will set the terms for you. Just keep in mind that having a court make the decision means there will be a trial, and that will cost you a lot of time and money.

The spouse who is ordered to pay alimony will usually have to pay a certain amount each month. Alimony continues for a set period of time that's defined in a judgment or settlement agreement, or until a certain event occurs, such as:

- the other spouse remarries
- the children no longer need a full-time parent at home
- a judge determines that after a reasonable period of time, the spouse receiving alimony has not made a sufficient effort to become at least partially self-supporting
- some other significant event—such as retirement—occurs, convincing a judge to modify the amount paid, or
- one of the spouses dies.

Taxes and Alimony

Alimony or spousal support is tax deductible for the person who makes the payments and taxable to the recipient.

If a Spouse Refuses to Pay Court-Ordered Alimony

If you secure an alimony order but your spouse refuses to make the required payments, take immediate legal action to enforce the order in court. Orders to pay monthly alimony have the same force as any other court order and, if handled properly, can be enforced with the very real possibility of obtaining regular payments. If necessary, a court may jail a stubborn ex-spouse to show that it means business.

Pets and Divorce

Legally, pets are property, and courts generally treat them as such at divorce, awarding them to one spouse as part of the property division. Recently, however, some judges have ordered shared ownership of pets, most often dogs.

Estate Planning After Divorce

During and after your divorce, it's important to take a close look at whom you've named, in wills or retirement plans, to inherit your property. (See Chapter 1 for more on estate planning.) It's very common, for example, for people to forget to change the beneficiary designation on a 401(k) plan—and as a result, for a big chunk of money to go to a former spouse when that wasn't the person's intention at all.

You should also review documents such as advance medical directives and powers of attorney (discussed in Chapter 7), to be sure your documents still reflect your wishes.

Changing Your Name After Divorce

If you took your spouse's name when you married, you may decide to keep it so that you have the same surname as your children or for another reason. Or you may decide not to keep your spouse's name. In most states, you can request that the judge handling your divorce make a formal order restoring your former or birth name. If your divorce decree contains such an order, that's all the paperwork you'll need. In some states, you can even have a completed divorce case reopened to provide for a name change. You'll probably want to get certified copies of the order as proof of the name change— check with the court clerk for details. Once you have the necessary documentation, you can use it to have your name changed on your identification and personal records.

If your divorce papers don't show your name change, you can usually still resume your former name without much fuss, especially if it's your birth name and you have a birth certificate to prove it. In many states, you can simply begin using your former name consistently and have it changed on all your personal records. However, if you run into problems because you've used your married name for many years, you might want to do a formal name change back to your original name so that it's very clear that it's your legal name.

RESOURCE

More information on changing your name. See www. nolo.com/legal-encyclopedia/name-change.

Changing Your Child's Name After Divorce

Traditionally, courts ruled that a father had an automatic right to have his child keep his last name if he continued to actively perform his parental role. But this is no longer true. Now a child's name may be changed by court petition if a judge concludes it is in the best interest of the child to do so. When deciding whether or not to grant a name change request, courts consider many factors, including: how long the current name has been used, the strength of the child's relationship with the parent who wants the name change, and the child's need to identify with a new family unit (if the change involves remarriage).

Keep in mind that even if your children's last name changes, it won't change the rights or duties of either parent regarding custody, visitation, child support, or inheritance rights.

RESOURCE

Helpful divorce books and websites:

- *Nolo's Essential Guide to Divorce*, by Emily Doskow (Nolo), is a thorough 50-state guide to the ins and outs of divorce, from how to handle key issues (alimony, child custody, and support) to drafting a marital settlement agreement and dividing property to working with lawyers and mediators. You can see the full table of contents and a sample chapter of this and other Nolo books at www.nolo.com.

- *Divorce After 50: Your Guide to the Unique Legal & Financial Challenges*, by Janice Green (Nolo), provides in-depth information on all key issues that older couples face.

- *Divorce Without Court: A Guide to Mediation & Collaborative Divorce,* by Katherine E. Stoner (Nolo), provides divorcing couples with all the information they need to work with a neutral third party to resolve differences and find solutions, or to participate in a collaborative process.
- *Divorce & Money: How to Make the Best Financial Decisions During Divorce,* by Violet Woodhouse with Matthew J. Perry (Nolo), explains the financial aspects of divorce.
- *Building a Parenting Agreement That Works: Child Custody Agreements Step by Step,* by Mimi Lyster Zemmelman (Nolo), walks you through the process of creating a complete parenting plan for your kids after your divorce.
- *Being a Great Divorced Father: Real-Life Advice From a Dad Who's Been There,* by Paul Mandelstein (Nolo), is a guide for divorced dads on how to stay connected to the kids and maintain a positive relationship with the ex.

For details on these products and more information on divorce, including useful articles and charts of state-by-state rules, see the Nolo website at www.nolo.com.

For state-specific information and advice, useful articles, support groups, forms and worksheets, and referrals to divorce professionals, see these websites:

- www.divorcenet.com
- www.divorcesupport.com
- www.divorceinfo.com
- www.divorcecentral.com, and
- www.womenslaw.org.

Child Custody

When parents split up, a key concern is always how they will share care of their children. In an ideal world, the parents, thinking only of what's best for their children, would discuss parenting arrangements and come up with a plan that ensured the children would have a stable environment and significant contact with both parents.

In reality, of course, that doesn't always happen. In many divorces, the questions of custody rights and parenting time turns into a huge battle involving lawyers, court-ordered custody evaluators, and huge amounts of time, money, and emotional stress—and the result is a court-imposed custody arrangement that no one is happy with. And who suffers the most from the escalation of acrimony and the waste of money? The children.

Fortunately, many courts are doing everything they can to steer parents toward a reasonably amicable negotiation over parenting issues. Most courts now require parents who are in conflict over parenting issues to attend mediation sessions with a family court employee or private mediator (a trained, neutral third party) to work something out that's truly in the best interests of the children. Only if that process doesn't work are the parents allowed to bring their conflict to court.

STATE RULES

State child custody rules. See the Divorce, Child Support & Child Custody section of Nolo's website (www.nolo.com/legal-encyclopedia/child-support).

Temporary Custody

When parents separate, they should come up with a temporary parenting agreement. It should cover the basics: who will stay in the family home, where the kids will stay when, and how much child support will be paid. (See Chapter 4 for details on child support.) It's a good idea to write down these agreements and include in the written agreement a statement that the arrangements are just temporary and that no one's agreeing to any permanent state of affairs. That way, you can take your time making a more long-term agreement, without worrying that agreeing to one thing now is going to bind you to it forever.

If parents can't agree on how to share time with the kids or who should have what type of custody, even on a temporary basis, the court will likely send them to mediation, where a trained mediator will try to get them to come to terms on temporary arrangements. (See the discussion of mediation below.) If that fails as well, the court will come up with a temporary custody arrangement that will be in place until the divorce is final. That process may take several hearings in court, which translates into a lot of money in lawyers' fees and an inevitable increase in bad feelings between the spouses.

A temporary custody agreement will remain in place until the judge approves a final judgment that includes permanent custody arrangements.

CAUTION

If you must take the kids and get out, get to court quickly. Family law judges frown on a parent who removes the children from the home without seeking the court's approval. A parent who must leave the family home quickly, perhaps because of domestic violence, should take the children along and, as quickly as possible, file a request in family court for temporary custody and child support. If you delay, the judge might order that the children be returned to the family home pending future proceedings to determine physical custody.

When Parents Decide on Custody: Parenting Agreements

Only a court can issue a custody order—but if parents can come up with their own custody and visitation agreement that works for the children, the court will be happy to approve it— meaning it will become a court order.

A parenting agreement is a detailed written agreement between divorcing parents that describes how they will deal with children's living arrangements, custodial time, holiday schedules, vacation, religion, travel, education, and other related issues. More and more, courts are encouraging the use of parenting agreements during divorce proceedings. If parents discuss and agree upon how to deal with issues affecting their children—rather than having the judge rule on those issues— they are more likely to stick to the terms of the agreement.

Parents may negotiate and write down a parenting agreement themselves, or seek the help of a child custody mediator, therapist, or another specialist. Once the agreement is complete, the judge must review it. As long as your parenting plan is reasonable, the court will approve it, perhaps as part of your final settlement agreement, and it will become an enforceable order. In other words, if your ex doesn't comply with its terms, you can return to court and ask the judge to order your former spouse to do so.

RESOURCE

More about making parenting agreements. *Building a Parenting Agreement That Works: Child Custody Agreements Step by Step*, by Mimi Lyster Zemmelman (Nolo), provides sample language and forms to create your own parenting agreement. You can see a full table of contents and a sample chapter at www.nolo.com.

Physical and Legal Custody

There are two types of custody: physical and legal. Physical custody means actually taking care of the children day to day—in other words, the child lives with the parent. Legal custody involves making decisions about a child's upbringing, such as medical care, education, and religion. Courts generally believe that it's best for children to have both parents responsible for legal decisions and, when possible, for both parents to share physical custody as well. That's why "joint custody," where parents share legal and physical custody, has become so common—and in some states the two types of custody are both encompassed in a custody award to one parent. However, it is possible in the majority of states for parents to share legal custody but for one parent to have sole or primary physical custody while the other parent has visitation rights.

Joint Custody

Parents with joint custody usually work out a schedule according to their work schedules, housing arrangements, and the children's needs. Kids may spend roughly equal amounts of time with both parents, or one parent may have significantly more parenting time—joint custody doesn't have to be exactly equal.

Joint physical custody works best if parents live fairly near each other, letting children maintain a normal routine. A common pattern is for children to split the week between each parent's home, although many other arrangements are possible, such as having the children spend weekends and holidays with one parent and weekdays with the other. There is even a joint custody arrangement called "bird's nest" custody, where the children remain in the family home and the parents take turns moving in and out, spending their out time in separate housing of their own. There's less disruption for the kids, but more hassle and expense for the parents.

Courts in every state are willing to order joint *legal* custody. In some states, courts automatically award joint legal custody unless the children's best interests—or a parent's health or safety—would be compromised. Many courts, however, are reluctant to order joint *physical* custody unless both parents agree to it and appear to be sufficiently able to communicate and cooperate with each other to make it work.

Sole Custody

In some cases, one parent may be granted sole physical custody. This could be because the other parent has moved away, is otherwise unavailable, or is abusive or neglectful. Except in cases of serious abuse, the noncustodial parent is usually given rights to regular visits with the children. (Visitation is discussed below.) Likewise, unless the noncustodial parent is abusive or the parents are completely unable to get along enough to make decisions together, the parents still share legal custody.

Split Custody

When a court grants custody of one child to one parent and another child to the other parent, it's called split custody. It's rare, but can happen if the court concludes it's in the best interest of the child. For example, when one parent moves after a divorce, a high school student might prefer to stay behind with the other parent in order to finish the last year of high school.

Visitation (Shared Parenting)

The term "visitation" is still widely used, but many professionals in the field of divorce and parenting—and many divorced parents themselves—feel that the word doesn't accurately describe the relationship between children and a noncustodial parent. Parents whose time with their kids is more limited are still parents, and when they are with their children, they are parenting, not visiting. Because the term is still commonly used, we'll use visitation here interchangeably with the terms "parenting time" or "shared parenting."

A court may award primary physical custody to one parent and give the other shared parenting time that is not considered joint custody. The parents then either work out a parenting schedule themselves or, if they can't agree, follow the schedule set by the court. To avoid arguments over missed visits and inconvenience, many courts encourage parents to work out a detailed parenting agreement that sets a parenting schedule and outlines details such as how vacations will be planned and how parents will deal with things like parent-teacher nights and sporting events. In extreme cases, a court may order supervised visitation or deny a parent any right to spend time with the kids.

Reasonable Visitation

Courts commonly give the noncustodial parent the right to "reasonable" visitation, leaving it to the parents to work out a precise schedule of time and place. This gives the parents flexibility to take into consideration both the parents' and the children's schedules. Practically speaking, however, a parent with sole physical custody has more control over the dates, times, and duration of visits. That parent isn't legally obligated to agree to any particular schedule, but judges do take note of cooperation. If you are uncooperative merely to vex your ex, it can backfire when you need to ask the court for something in the future.

For the reasonable visitation approach to succeed, parents need to cooperate and communicate frequently. If you suspect that a loosely defined schedule won't work, insist on a fixed one. If you've already agreed to reasonable visitation and it isn't working out—for example, one parent is consistently late, skips scheduled visits, or doesn't provide enough information about where the kids are and what they are doing—you can go back to court and ask that the arrangement be changed.

Fixed Visitation

Sometimes courts set up a detailed visitation schedule, including the times and places for visitation with the noncustodial parent—for example, every other weekend. A court will be inclined to order a fixed schedule if the hostility between the parents is so severe that the regular contact between them may be detrimental to the child. A fixed visitation schedule can still be generous, but it removes opportunities for one party to control the other's time and gives the children predictability in an often unsettling period.

Supervised Visitation

When a noncustodial parent has a history of violent or destructive behavior, especially toward the child, or past problems with drugs and alcohol, the court may require that visits between that parent and the child be supervised. This means that an adult (other than the custodial parent) must be present at all times. The adult may be someone the parents agree on or someone appointed by the court. No matter how the supervising adult is chosen, the court must approve the person.

Grandparents' Visitation Rights

All states have some laws allowing grandparents to ask a court for the legal right to maintain a relationship with their grandchildren. But state laws vary greatly when it comes to the crucial details, such as who can visit and under what circumstances.

Many states have "restrictive" visitation statutes, meaning that grandparents can get a court order for visitation only if the child's parents are divorcing or if one or both parents have died. States with more permissive visitation laws allow courts to consider a visitation request even without the death of a parent or the dissolution of the family, as long as visitation would serve the best interests of the child. The children's welfare is always the highest priority, although the courts also give great deference to a parent's decision to limit visitation with grandparents, and in most places, when parents agree that they don't want the grandparents to visit the kids, that's usually the end of the story.

Stepparents' and Others' Visitation Rights

In most states, someone who has helped to raise a child but has no legal relationship to the child—a stepparent, for example—has few legal rights to seek custody or even visitation. If you have been actively involved in a child's life but are not a legal parent, try to work out an arrangement with the child's custodial parent to continue that role. If that's not possible, check your state laws on visitation rights or consult a family law attorney.

Custody Decisions When Spouses Are in Different States

If parents live in different states, which state's courts are in charge of custody decisions? These questions are determined by laws called the Uniform Child Custody Jurisdiction Act (UCCJA) or the Uniform Child Custody Jurisdiction and Enforcement Act (UCCJEA), one of which has been adopted by every state and the District of Columbia.

In general, a state may make a custody decision about a child only if one of these tests is met (in order of preference):

- The state is the child's home state. This means the child has lived in the state for the last six months or was living there but is absent because a parent took the child to another state. A parent who wrongfully removes or retains a child in order to create a home state will be denied custody.

- The child has significant connections in the state with people such as teachers, doctors, and grandparents. A parent who wrongfully removes or keeps a child in order to establish these significant connections will be denied custody.

- The child is in the state and either has been abandoned or is in danger of being abused or neglected if sent back to the previous home state.

- No other state can meet one of the first three tests, or a state that can meet at least one has declined to make a custody decision.

If a state cannot meet one of these tests, the courts of that state cannot make a custody award, even if the child is present in the state. If more than one state meets one of the tests, any of them may make a custody decision; to decide which one, judges in the different states will confer and make a decision. Once a state makes a custody award, other states must stay out of the dispute.

How Courts Rule on Custody: The Best Interests of the Child

If divorcing parents agree on a parenting plan that appears reasonable, the judge will usually approve it. But if parents are fighting and the court must make parenting decisions, almost all states require judges to base custody decisions on the best interests of the child. Laws in nearly every state provide guidelines on this standard, although judges have a lot of discretion in interpreting them.

Courts commonly consider:

- the child's age, sex, and mental and physical health
- each parent's mental and physical health
- each parent's lifestyle (such as a new live-in relationship) and other social factors, including whether the child is exposed to secondhand smoke or drug use in the home and whether there is any history of child or spousal abuse
- the emotional bond between each parent and the child, as well as each parent's ability to give the child guidance
- each parent's ability to provide food, shelter, clothing, and medical care
- the child's established living pattern (school, home, community, and religious institution)
- the quality of the child's education in the current situation
- the child's preference, if the child is old enough to weigh the alternatives (children's opinions are usually considered once they reach the age of 12 or so), and
- the ability and willingness of each parent to foster healthy communication and contact between the child and the other parent.

In some states, conservative judges will also consider factors like sexual orientation and whether a parent is cohabiting with a new partner, whether of the same or the opposite sex. (There's more about sexual orientation and same-sex parents below.)

If none of these factors clearly favors one parent, most courts tend to focus on which parent is likely to provide the children a more stable environment, and which parent will better foster the child's relationship with the other parent. With younger children, this may mean awarding custody to the parent who has been the child's primary caregiver. With older children, this may mean giving custody to the parent who is best able to foster continuity in education, neighborhood life, religious institutions, and peer relationships.

Expert Help

Often, judges need help in making custody decisions and determining what's in the child's best interests. Depending on state law and local custom, judges may:

- require the parents to meet with a mediator, who will then make a recommendation (see the discussion of mediation below)
- appoint an investigator or custody evaluator (often a mental health professional or social worker) to visit the parents' homes and talk with the parents and, if appropriate, the children, or
- appoint an attorney to represent the child, in cases where the conflict is so extreme that it's clear neither parent is capable of considering the child's needs and another adult must step in to advise the judge on best interests.

Court Preference for Awarding Custody to Mothers

In the past, it was very common for courts to award custody of children of "tender years" (five and under) to the mother when parents divorced. This rule has been rejected in most states, or relegated to the role of tiebreaker if two fit parents request custody of their preschool children. In most states, courts determine custody based only on the children's best interests, without regard to the sex of the parent. Even without a court order, many divorcing parents with young children agree that the mother will have sole or at least primary physical custody, with the father spending time with the children according to a reasonable schedule, generally increasing as the children get older.

When a Parent Moves Away

A parent who moves out and leaves the children with the other parent may have trouble getting custody switched back at a later date. Even when a parent leaves to avoid a dangerous or highly unpleasant situation, leaving the children there sends a message to the court that the other parent is a suitable choice for physical custody. Also, assuming the children stay in the home where the parents lived as a family, continue in the same school, and participate in their usual activities, a judge may be reluctant to move them, if only to avoid disrupting the children's routines.

Religion and Child Custody

Even when they are married, parents of different faiths don't always agree on whose religion the children will follow. When parents separate, things can get even more complicated. Courts that are called upon to resolve disputes about the religious upbringing of children have a difficult job in trying to balance the competing concerns of:

- a parent's First Amendment right to the free exercise of religion, as well as the right to raise children as the parent sees fit (as long as the choices do not endanger the child), and
- the best interests of the child.

There is no uniform national law on the subject. Instead, the law varies from state to state and even from court to court. Some courts allow each parent to practice that parent's religion during custodial time; others believe it's better for children to have a consistent religious education and allow the parent with primary custody to make the decisions, prohibiting the other parent from interfering.

Sexual Orientation and Child Custody

Only the District of Columbia has a law on its books stating that a parent's sexual orientation cannot be the sole factor in making a custody or visitation award. In a few states—including Alaska, California, New Mexico, and Pennsylvania—courts have ruled that a parent's homosexuality, in and of itself, cannot be grounds for an automatic denial of custody or visitation rights. In many other states, courts have ruled that judges can deny custody or visitation because of a parent's sexual orientation only if they find that the parent's sexual orientation would harm the child.

In reality, however, a lesbian, gay, bisexual, or transgender (LGBT) parent can still face a difficult struggle when trying to gain custody in many courtrooms, especially if that parent lives with a partner. This is because judges, when considering the best interests of the child, may be motivated by their own or community prejudices and may find reasons other than the lesbian or gay parent's sexual orientation to deny custody or appropriate visitation. Any LGBT parent who is involved in a contested custody battle should contact an experienced attorney for help.

Custody by Someone Other Than a Parent

Sometimes neither parent can safely assume custody of the children, perhaps because of substance abuse or a mental health problem. In these situations, a court will give custody of the children to someone other than a parent—often, a grandparent—who becomes the child's legal guardian. If relatives aren't available, the child may be sent to a foster home or public facility.

Same-Sex Parents and Custody

For parents of the same sex who are married or registered in a marriage equivalent state (see Chapter 1 regarding same-sex relationships), issues of custody will be pretty much the same as for opposite-sex couples. The court will respect both parents' rights and make custody and visitation decisions on the basis of the child's best interests.

However, it's more complicated when only one parent in a same-sex couple has legal rights. This is a fairly common occurrence—sometimes one partner adopts as a single person to avoid homophobic adoption rules; sometimes a lesbian mom gives birth in a state where the couple's relationship isn't recognized so that her partner isn't considered a legal parent; sometimes a couple gets together after a child is born and the second parent isn't a legal parent. The courts are all over the map on the custody and visitation rights of the second parent in these cases. In some states, courts have held that a person who has established a psychological parent-child relationship with a partner's biological child is entitled to visitation and, in some cases, to legal status as a parent. In other places, courts have shut out nonbiological parents entirely based on the absence of a genetic or legal relationship with the child. The law is certainly not settled, and the best course of action is usually to try to mediate an agreement rather than going to court and fighting over kids you have raised together. There's more about mediation below.

SEE AN EXPERT

Get expert help for custody questions. If you are involved in a custody case and concerned about bias against you because you are gay or lesbian, consult an attorney. You can get attorney names from the National Center for Lesbian Rights (www.nclrights.org, phone 800-528-6257) or Lambda Legal (www. lambdalegal.org, phone 212-809-8585).

RESOURCE

Help for gay and lesbian parents. *A Legal Guide for Lesbian & Gay Couples,* by Frederick Hertz and Emily Doskow (Nolo), has advice on negotiating custody arrangements. *Making It Legal: A Guide to Same-Sex Marriage, Domestic Partnerships & Civil Unions,* by Frederick Hertz with Emily Doskow (Nolo), explains the law in different states and covers parenting issues. You can see the full table of contents and a sample chapter for each book at www.nolo.com.

Mediating Child Custody and Visitation Disputes

Mediation can often help divorcing parents resolve parenting arrangements with a minimum of hard feelings and expense. It's a nonadversarial process during which a neutral person, the mediator, meets with the parents to help them negotiate custody and visitation issues. Mediators are very skilled at getting parents—even those with a lot of bitterness over the divorce—to cooperate and work out a parenting plan for the sake of their children.

Most states require mediation in custody and visitation disputes, and others allow courts to order mediation. Whenever mediation is required by the court, the court will direct the parents to a mediator—in some places, the services will be free to the parents, but in many courts parents must pay if they can. Parents can also find and pay a private mediator themselves—either a family law attorney, a therapist with expertise in custody disputes, or even a nonlawyer mediator from a community mediation service.

A mediator does not have power to impose a solution on divorcing parents, but instead helps them reach an agreement. If the attempt fails and parents still can't agree on custody, the court will decide. In some states, the mediator can report to the judge about the mediation process and can make a recommendation about what the judge should decide, but most states consider discussions in mediation sessions to be confidential, meaning the mediator can't talk to the judge about them and can't be asked to testify in court.

Mediation is superior to litigation for resolving custody and visitation disputes for several reasons:

- **It's less expensive.** If you go to trial over custody issues, you'll end up paying lawyers (and possibly, expert witnesses) huge amounts. A custody trial could easily cost $10,000 to $20,000.
- **It's faster.** Mediation usually produces a settlement after five to ten hours of mediation over a week or two. Child custody litigation can drag on for months or even years.
- **It's easier on everyone.** Mediation enhances communication between parents and makes it much more likely that they will be able to cooperate on child-raising issues after the divorce. Experts who have studied the effects of divorce on children universally conclude that children suffer far less when divorcing or separating parents cooperate.

RESOURCE

Good mediation resources:

- Both www.mediate.com and www.acrnet.org (the website of a national mediation organization called the Association for Conflict Resolution) can help you find a mediator in your area.

- *Divorce Without Court: A Guide to Mediation & Collaborative Divorce,* by Katherine E. Stoner (Nolo), is a useful guide to mediation in divorce cases. See www.nolo. com for a full table of contents and sample chapter.

Changing Custody and Visitation Orders

After a court issues a final divorce decree or another order establishing a parenting plan, it's always possible to modify the order if circumstances change. However, parents can't just come in and ask for a change because they don't like the current arrangement; there has to be some significant change in either the parent's situation or the children's in order to get a court to agree to modify existing arrangements. (See below for examples.)

If the parents agree on a change to their existing parenting schedule, they can agree to a modification. If they included a provision in their final judgment to this effect, then they can just write down their new agreement, sign it, and consider it a part of the judgment just as if a judge had reviewed it. However, not all final judgments contain such a provision.

If there isn't one, the parents can go into court—generally the same court that decided the original divorce and custody plan—and ask the court to approve their new agreement. This will ensure that if one parent later reneges on the agreement, the other person will be able to enforce it. If both parents agree, courts will approve their modification agreement unless the court concludes it isn't in the best interests of the child.

If a parent wants to change an existing court order and the other parent won't agree to the change, the parent who wants the change must submit a written request to the court that issued the order, showing a significant change in circumstances; for example, if either parent wants to move a significant distance from where the children live.

Custodial Interference

In most states, it's a crime for one parent to take a child from the other with the intent to interfere with that parent's physical custody of the child. This crime is commonly referred to as "custodial interference." The police will become involved to get the child returned and arrest the parent who took the child. In most states, the parent deprived of custody may also sue the other person for money damages.

It's even more serious if a parent without physical custody (whether the parent has visitation rights or not) removes a child from—or refuses to return a child to—the parent with physical custody. This is kidnapping or child concealment—a felony in most states.

In many states, it's also a felony to take a child out of state with the intent of interfering with a parent's custody. Many states, however, recognize good-cause defenses—for example, if a mother took a child to prevent imminent bodily harm to herself or to the child. In addition, some states let a parent take a child out of state if the parent is requesting custody in court and has notified the court or police of the child's location.

RESOURCE

International custody disputes. The International Child Abductions Remedies Act is a federal law that covers child custody disputes involving other countries. See the Office of Children's Issues in the U.S. State Department (www.travel. state.gov/abduction) for details on international parental child abduction.

Custody Issues Involving Unmarried Parents

Parents who are not married have the same parental rights as those who are. The concept of "illegitimacy" has pretty much gone by the wayside, and all children are considered legitimate whether their parents are married or not. When an opposite-sex married couple with children breaks up, they are subject to the same laws as married parents relating to their parenting arrangements. They will use a slightly different procedure to get the matter before the court: It will not be a divorce, but a parentage action in which they legally establish the parent-child relationship and then ask the court to make—or affirm—decisions about shared parenting.

Unmarried couples of the same sex deal with different issues. See "Same-Sex Parents and Custody," above.

Surrogacy and Custody

As more and more couples face infertility issues, the use of surrogacy has become more popular. In the most common type of surrogacy arrangement, a gestational surrogate agrees to implantation in her womb of an embryo that was created from genetic material from either the intended parents or egg and sperm donors. In other words, the surrogate herself has no genetic connection to the resulting child, but carries the child to term on behalf of the intended parents. (In a so-called "traditional" surrogacy, the surrogate's own eggs are used, but this results in the surrogate's being considered a legal parent in most states, which creates legal complications. Thus, traditional surrogacy is much less common.)

Typically, the surrogate receives a fee for her gestational services, along with reimbursement for all medical and other expenses associated with the pregnancy. It is, of course, illegal to sell either a child or genetic material, so the surrogacy contract must make clear that the payment is for services and expenses, not for the surrogate's giving up the child. Surrogacy contracts are lengthy and complex, and surrogacy is not legal everywhere.

In places where surrogacy is legal and a valid contract is in place, the contract will usually be enforced by the courts even if the surrogate tries to break the contract and keep the baby.

RESOURCE

More on state surrogacy laws. For details on the laws in your state, see the website of the Human Rights Campaign at www.hrc.org (search for "surrogacy laws") or call 800-777-4723. You'll also find useful information on surrogacy at Resolve (the National Infertility Association) website www.resolve.org (click on "Family Building Options," then "Surrogacy"), or call 703-556-7172.

RESOURCE

Custody resource in your state. The site www. womenslaw.org offers excellent plain-English explanations of state custody rules. Also, *Nolo's Essential Guide to Child Custody & Support*, by Emily Doskow (Nolo), provides step-by-step guidance on child custody, from choosing a plan to enforcing (or changing) child support. The book includes 50-state resources on custody and child support laws.

CHAPTER

Child Support

Divorce doesn't affect parents' obligation to support their children—every parent has that obligation from the moment a child is born until the child turns 18, and sometimes longer. Part of the divorce process will be a determination of whether support will be paid, by whom, and how much; generally, all of these things are determined by state guidelines.

Unfortunately, too many parents simply don't make good on their child support obligations. Some don't have the money, but some choose not to make payments for a variety of their own reasons—none of which will get them off the hook, legally. Parents who truly can't make their payments, perhaps because they're out of work, can always go back to court and ask for a change in the amount in light of their changed circumstances.

It is the children, of course, who suffer the most when child support is inadequate or nonexistent. Recognizing this, the trend in all states is to increase child support levels and implement new ways to enforce child support obligations.

 STATE RULES

State child support rules. See the Divorce, Child Support & Child Custody section of Nolo's website (www.nolo.com/legal-encyclopedia/child-support).

Who Must Pay Child Support

All parents—biological or adoptive, married or not—have a duty to support their children. You're not obligated to support stepchildren (the children of your spouse) unless you legally adopt them.

What does support mean? Parents must provide their children with food, shelter, clothing, and whatever education is required by state law. They are not obligated to provide material goods beyond that.

Courts don't intervene in how parents support their children unless children are being abused or neglected. However, when couples separate or divorce, courts will step in with orders about what parents must do to support the children. Or, if a single mother applies for financial assistance from a social services agency, the agency will do everything possible to get reimbursement from the children's father and to establish a child support order so that he's responsible for paying support instead of the government having to do it.

Divorcing Parents

Many divorcing parents work out temporary support payments while the divorce is pending, based on their family budgets, the parents' incomes, and the temporary parenting arrangement. Almost all judges and divorce lawyers use special software to calculate child support using state guidelines, which are usually too mathematically complex to allow for calculations by hand. Parents can work with a lawyer or mediator, use Internet calculators to get a ballpark idea of their state's guidelines for child support (discussed below), or simply work out what they think is fair. It's to both parents' advantage to write down the temporary support agreement and have the court approve it and enter it as an order. The receiving parent can then feel secure that the court can enforce payments if the paying parent bails out, and the paying parent can be secure in the amount that's agreed to, at least until it's time to enter a longer term order.

Parents who can't come to an agreement about support will find themselves in front of a judge—and that is an enormous waste of money and time, because the judge will simply order guideline support, which the parents could have figured out for themselves or had a lawyer or mediator calculate for them for a much lower cost than a contested hearing.

Child support guidelines use a formula to calculate support based on each parent's percentage of time spent with the children, each parent's income, which parent takes dependent exemptions and what each parent's filing status is, which parent pays for the children's health insurance and child care, and other financial factors. When a couple finalizes their divorce, they'll either agree to continue the temporary support amount that was being paid while the divorce was pending or settle on a permanent amount going forward. "Permanent" doesn't mean it can never be changed, just that it's part of the final judgment of divorce. (See "Modifying Child Support Payments," below.)

Mothers and fathers have an equal duty to support their children and an equal right to receive child support from the other parent if circumstances warrant it. A father with physical custody of a child has the right to ask the other parent for child support, just as a mother with physical custody does.

Unmarried Parents

If you're a parent, you're responsible for supporting your child whether or not you were ever married to the child's other parent, and whether or not a court ever ordered you to support the child. It's just part of being a parent. The court will use the same guidelines for unmarried parents as for married ones.

If a child is born to married parents, the husband is presumed to be the child's father. But if the mother is unmarried when a child is born, it may not be clear, legally, who the father is. Many unmarried fathers acknowledge paternity by signing a voluntary declaration of paternity at the time of the child's birth or soon after. Some states require such a statement of paternity before they will add an unmarried father's name to a child's birth certificate. It's also possible for a man who never married the child's mother to be presumed to be the father if he welcomes the child into his home and openly holds the child out as his own.

If a man believed to be a child's father resists taking responsibility, either the mother—or the state, on behalf of an agency paying support to an unwed mother—can file a paternity action to prove that he is the father, and if he is, the next step will be an action for child support. Sometimes the government catches up with the father many years later, and he is required to pay thousands of dollars in back support that he never knew he owed.

Establishing Paternity

A paternity lawsuit, to determine the identity of the father of a child born outside of marriage, may be brought either by the mother or by the father himself if the mother is denying his paternity. Paternity is usually proved by genetic testing. Once it's established, the father has all the rights and obligations of parenthood, including the duty to support the child and the right to ask a court for custody or visitation.

How Child Support Obligations Are Calculated

Each state has guidelines for calculating child support, based primarily on the parents' incomes and the amount of time each parent spends with the children. These guidelines (a requirement of the federal Child Support Enforcement Act), vary considerably from state to state. In addition, guidelines in some states give judges considerable leeway in setting the actual amount. But an increasing number of states impose strict guidelines that leave judges very little latitude.

RESOURCE

State guidelines and information on child support rules:

- www.alllaw.com/calculators/childsupport offers child support calculators for each state. Parents can go online and get a ballpark idea of what guideline support would be in their state.

- www.ncsea.org, the website of the National Child Support Enforcement Association, has contact information for every state child support enforcement agency. See the section "For Parents" under the Resources & Info tab.

- www.supportguidelines.com provides an extensive list of links to state and federal laws and agencies.

Factors That Affect Child Support Payments

Most state guidelines use similar factors to determine who pays child support, and how much. These factors usually include:

- each parent's net income
- the time the children spend with each parent
- the number, ages, and needs of the children—including health insurance, education, day care, and special needs
- the family's predivorce standard of living, and
- hardship factors that affect a parent's ability to pay support (see below).

It's very common for parents to agree on child support after doing some research online or having a brief consultation with an attorney, because there's not all that much leeway in the guidelines. In other words, it's not really worth it to fight about it because the guidelines dictate a result and courts don't deviate from that result very often. If parents aren't able to reach a compromise and bring their dispute to the judge, courts often require each divorcing spouse to fill out a financial statement that gives a complete picture of the parents' financial situations. Even when parents do agree, each parent must detail monthly income and expenses for the court, so that the judge can evaluate whether the amount of support is appropriate.

How Courts Evaluate a Parent's Ability to Pay Child Support

The numbers used to calculate guideline support start with each parent's net income. Net income is gross income from all sources—such as wages, investment income, rental income from real estate, or public benefits—minus mandatory deductions, such as income taxes, Social Security tax, union dues, and health care costs.

When figuring net income, most courts don't consider voluntary deductions from a parent's paycheck, such as 401(k) contributions, or loan or credit card payments deducted automatically. Nor do they give credit for wage attachments, which generally mean that a portion of the person's wages are being withheld to pay off a debt or, possibly, to pay support for children from another marriage. (However, in some states, courts do allow a deduction for the amount of child support paid for other children.)

When calculating guideline support, most courts do not deduct reasonable expenses for the necessities of life—for example, rent, mortgage, food, clothing, and health care, and they almost never include expenses such as tuition, eating in restaurants, or entertainment. The idea is that parents' support of their children should have a higher priority than personal expenses. If expenses for necessities are particularly high for some reason, parents must ask the court to deviate from guideline support and take those factors into account. Otherwise, it's assumed that guideline support takes basic living expenses into account.

In most states, the judge is authorized to examine a parent's ability to earn as well as what the parent is actually earning, and to impute income and order child support payments based on the ability to make more income. Say, for example, a father with an obligation to pay child support leaves his current job and takes a lower-paying job that he likes better because it's more creative or less stressful. In this situation, a court may base the child support on the income from the original job (ability to earn) rather than on the new income level (ability to pay). The children's current needs take priority over the parent's career plans and desires. However, if income is reduced because a parent decides to go back to school for a degree that is likely to increase the parent's earning capacity, the court may be more flexible in setting support.

How Long Child Support Lasts

In general, state laws require that all parents support their child until:

- the child reaches the age of majority (this varies by state, but is usually 18) and sometimes longer if the child has special needs or is in college
- the child is on active military duty
- the biological parents' rights and responsibilities are terminated—for example, when a child is adopted by someone else, or
- the child has been declared emancipated by a court and has the legal rights of an adult (see Chapter 6 for details on emancipation).

In some divorce settlement agreements, the parents set a specific date to terminate child support—usually after the child finishes college or otherwise becomes self-supporting. If there's no such agreement, state law governs the date that support ends.

When a Parent Falls Behind on Child Support Payments

Each installment of court-ordered child support is due on a specific date set out in the divorce or parentage order from the court. Overdue payments are called arrearages or arrears—and federal and state governments take an aggressive approach to collecting them.

Back Child Support: It Never Goes Away

Once child support is owed, it is owed until the parent pays it in full. Even filing for bankruptcy, which wipes out many debts, does not cancel child support debt. A parent who's fallen behind on payments can ask a judge to lower future payments (see "Modifying Child Support Payments," below), but that doesn't affect the past due amount, which must be paid in full. In fact, judges in most states are prohibited by law from retroactively modifying a child support obligation.

 TIP

If you fall behind, immediately go to court and request a temporary modification of your payment amount. If you just let payments slide, you'll be on the hook for a debt you might not ever be able to pay off.

Collecting Delinquent Child Support Payments

All child support orders contain automatic wage assignment orders, meaning that a portion of the paying parent's paycheck can be taken and sent directly to the recipient parent if the receiving parent opts to use the wage assignment. (Some don't— if they're not worried about nonpayment, it is just as easy to have the paying parent send a check directly, and it keeps the employer out of the paying parent's personal life.) However, in order to get your money this way, you must provide the employer with the court order. And a wage assignment won't work for self-employed parents or those whose income is more sporadic.

Every state has a child support enforcement agency with the job of helping parents, whether married or unmarried, collect overdue child support. (They'll even help if the paying parent has moved out of state, as required by the Uniform Interstate Family Support Act.) These efforts might range from meeting with the ex-spouse and arranging a payment schedule to contacting an employer and getting money withheld (garnished) from every paycheck. All child support orders from a court include a wage garnishment order—cooperative parents usually don't enforce it, but if you're having trouble getting your support payments, you can use it. To garnish wages, you'll need to send the court order on child support (and some other paperwork) to your ex's employer, who will then deduct child support payments from every paycheck. The child support enforcement agency will help you do this, and most of these services are free or low cost. The website of the National Child Support Enforcement Association (www.ncsea.org) has contact information for every state child support enforcement agency.

State and federal governments and agencies may also withhold federal income tax refunds, deny a passport, and suspend or restrict a business, occupational, or driver's license when a parent is delinquent in paying child support. Once a state child support enforcement agency has listed a parent as delinquent, these actions will happen automatically the next time a license comes up for renewal or the parent applies for a passport. As a last resort, the court that issued the child support order can hold a delinquent parent in contempt of court and, in the absence of a reasonable explanation for the delinquency, impose a jail term. Jail terms aren't common, because courts would rather see the parent working and earning money to pay the support—but a parent who has repeatedly flouted court orders and failed to pay significant arrearages may see the inside of a jail cell.

Tracking Down Out-of-State Parents

If your children's other parent has moved out of state, you can use legal procedures, either on your own or with the help of your state's child support enforcement agency, to locate your ex and seek payment of current support as well as arrearages. You have several options, including:

- asking a court in your state to force the parent to pay (as long as your state has legal authority over the parent; if you got your divorce there, then the state has that authority, called jurisdiction)
- ask a court in your state to forward the current child support order, as well as any new orders made on arrearages, to a court in the state where your ex lives, and have that state's courts and agencies enforce the order
- file an enforcement request directly in the state where the other parent lives by contacting that state's child support enforcement agency or hiring a local attorney, or
- forward the support order to the other parent's employer and ask the employer to withhold the support amounts

from paychecks. However, if there are significant arrearages, you may need to go back to court to get an order for a higher wage assignment to cover both current and past-due support.

Finding a Delinquent Parent's Assets

The federal government tracks a delinquent parent's assets with resources such as the Federal Parent Locator Services, which is a government service designed to help parents collect past-due child support and enforce child support payments. Federal law also requires employers to report all new hires to their state's child support enforcement agency (the Personal Responsibility and Work Opportunity Reconciliation Act of 1996, or PRWORA). The agency then forwards this data to the National Directory of New Hires, a centralized registry that searches lists of new employees for parents who owe child support and quickly sets up wage withholding orders for these delinquent parents. Under PRWORA, financial institutions—such as banks, savings and loans, credit unions, insurance companies, and money market funds—must also search the account records of parents who owe child support. When a match is identified, the information is sent to the state within 48 hours, so the accounts can be seized.

RESOURCE

State child support enforcement agencies and information on programs and options for collecting (and

paying) child support. See the website of the National Child Support Enforcement Association, www.ncsea.org, or call 703-506-2880. You'll find information about the Federal Parent Locator Service at www.acf.hhs.gov/programs/css/fpls.

Modifying Child Support Payments

You and your child's other parent may agree to increase or decrease child support amounts—and if there's a significant change in either parent's situation, it's a good idea to figure out something that will work for both of you, rather than spending time and money in court. However, even if you reach an agreement, make sure you write it down and have a judge approve it. If it's not approved by a judge, meaning that it becomes a court order, then the paying parent still owes the original support amount, and the recipient parent can try to collect the full amount even after agreeing to a lesser amount. If you had a lawyer for your divorce, you can ask the same lawyer to help you with a support modification—or you can try doing it yourself using your court's self-help materials.

If one parent wants a change and the other won't agree, the parent seeking the modification must ask the court to hold a hearing, at which each of you can argue your side. As a general rule, the court will not modify an existing order unless the parent proposing the modification can show changed circumstances— for example, a job layoff that resulted in lower income. This rule encourages stability and helps prevent the court from becoming overburdened with frequent modification requests. If the court does order a modification, depending on the circumstances, it may be temporary or permanent.

Temporary Modification

Changed circumstances that could support a temporary modification include a child's medical emergency, a temporary inability to pay—for instance, because of a medical emergency or an involuntary job loss, or a temporary increase in need—commonly from some kind of economic or medical hardship—on the part of the parent receiving support.

Permanent Modification

A judge may permanently modify a child support order under one of the following circumstances: either parent receives additional income from remarriage, changes in the child support laws, job change of either parent, cost of living increase, disability of either parent, or changes in the needs of the child.

A permanently modified child support order will remain in effect until child support is no longer required or the order is modified again.

Child Support and Taxes

Child support doesn't have any tax consequences for either the paying parent or the receiving parent—it's neither taxable nor deductible. (This is different from spousal support, or alimony, which is tax deductible for the person who makes the payments and taxable to the recipient.)

Which Payments Are Child Support?

To qualify as child support, payments must be designated as child support in a divorce or separation agreement. If the agreement lumps the payments together as "family support" or "alimony" and doesn't designate a specific portion of each payment as child support, *none* of the payment will be considered child support for tax purposes. This can have adverse tax consequences for both the payer and the recipient of child support payments, because family support or alimony is taxable to the recipient, and the paying parent won't get the tax deduction either.

Who Gets to Claim a Child as a Dependent

When parents divorce or separate, only one of them can claim the dependent exemption each year for any given child. The IRS will come down hard if both try to claim it; the agency cross-references dependents' Social Security numbers to make sure taxpayers don't get away with this.

During a divorce, it can be unclear who is entitled to take the exemption when both parents are supporting the child and are sharing custody. The IRS rule is this: If parents lived apart during the entire last six months of the calendar year, or if they have a written divorce decree, maintenance agreement, or separation agreement, *and* more than half of the child's total support for the year came from one or both parents (the rest can come from relatives or public benefits), *and* the child was in the custody of one or both parents during the year, then the parent who had custody for the greater part of the year gets the exemption.

However, the parents may agree to give the exemption to the noncustodial parent if either of the following is true:

- In the divorce decree or separation agreement, the custodial parent gave up (waived) the right to claim the dependent exemption.
- The custodial parent signs a declaration (IRS Form 8332) relinquishing the right to claim the dependent exemption, and the noncustodial parent attaches this declaration to that year's tax return. Using this form, the custodial parent can relinquish the exemption for one year, a number of years, or forever.

If you relinquish the exemption, you also give up eligibility for the child tax credit (discussed in Chapter 6).

If the parents are not married, did not live apart during the last six months of the calendar year, or do not have a written agreement about support and custody, then the parent who provides more than 50% of a child's support during the tax year can claim the child as a dependent.

RESOURCE

Information on taxes and child support payments.
See IRS Publication 504, *Divorced or Separated Individuals*, which you can download for free from www.irs.gov.

Adoption

CHAPTER 5

Adoption, no less than birth, is a profound event. Like birth, it creates a new parent-child bond and changes the makeup of the family. Once an adoption is complete, the new parent-child relationship is recognized for all purposes, including child support obligations, inheritance rights, and custody.

All states have very specific and exacting rules governing the adoption process, and the Interstate Compact on the Placement of Children governs adoptions that involve a child crossing state lines. Every adoption must be approved by a court in the state where the adopting parents live. Birth parents must consent to the adoption, and adoptive parents must be fit to take on this most important responsibility. And most important, the court must rule that the adoption is in the best interests of the child.

Who Can Adopt

Anyone who wishes to adopt must be a fit parent in the eyes of the court that's charged with approving or denying an adoption request. Before the court makes that determination, however, some states impose certain threshold requirements on adoptive parents:

- **Residence.** A few states or local counties require the adoptive parent to live in the state for a certain length of time before adopting. The residency period is usually a year or less.

- **Marital status.** Most states allow single people and unmarried couples to adopt, but a few do ban adoption by unmarried people petitioning together. Courts, adoption agencies, and birth parents, however, often favor heterosexual married couples. Unmarried singles or couples may have to wait longer to adopt or be flexible about the child they can adopt; it may be easier to adopt an older child or one with special needs.

- **Sexual orientation.** Only Utah and Mississippi prohibit openly gay people from adopting. An increasing number of states allow same-sex partners who are legally married or registered in a marriage equivalent relationship to adopt a partner's child. Courts in 21 states and the District of Columbia have ruled that a gay couple may adopt a child together when neither is the child's biological or legal parent, and other states allow it although there are no laws explicitly permitting it. (See "Same-Sex Couples and Adoption," below.)

- **Race or ethnicity.** Adoptive parents do not need to be of the same race as the child, but some states give preference to prospective adoptive parents of the same race or ethnic background as the child; sometimes these preferences take the form of state laws, and sometimes they are policies of the state adoption agencies. Adoptions of Native American children are governed by special rules and procedures set out in a federal law, the Indian Child Welfare Act.

- **Age.** Most states require an adoptive parent to be ten or more years older than the child.

In addition to state rules, private adoption agencies may impose their own additional requirements or preferences, as long as the rules don't violate state antidiscrimination laws. (See "Agency Adoptions," below.)

Special Challenges of Single-Parent Adoptions

If you're a single person wishing to adopt, be prepared to make a good case for your fitness as a parent. When you apply to an agency to be matched with a birth parent, you can expect questions about why you haven't married, how you plan to support and care for a child on your own, what will happen if you do marry, and other questions that will put you in the position of defending your status as a single person. If you are accepted by the agency, you may face similar questions from prospective birth parents concerned about giving up their child to a single parent, and it may take longer to find a match.

The Birth Parents' Consent

For an adoption to be legal, in most instances, both birth parents must consent to it. Once a birth parent's consent is final, the birth parent gives up all parental rights, including the right to visit the child or make decisions regarding the child's life. Birth parents often have a great deal of control over who adopts their child: Commonly, with private agency and independent adoptions, birth parents choose the adoptive parents. The birth parents may also work out an arrangement with the adoptive parents so that they have continuing contact with the child—called an open adoption.

RESOURCE

More on legal rights of birth parents. The Child Welfare Information Gateway includes useful articles on the legal rights of birth parents intending to place a child for adoption. See www.childwelfare.gov/adoption/birth/for or call 800-394-3366.

Who Must Consent

Both birth parents must consent to an adoption—a birth mother can't place a child for adoption without the consent of the child's presumed father. A presumed father is a man who was married to the child's mother at the time the baby was born, who put his name on a child's birth certificate, or who behaved like a father, including taking the child into his home and saying that he was the child's father. This legal presumption can be overruled if it's demonstrated by genetic testing that someone else is the child's biological father, but unless that happens, the presumed father has a right to be notified of any adoption proceeding and to either consent or object.

In some states, there's also a category called an alleged or putative father—someone who doesn't meet any of these requirements but who says he is the father or is identified by the birth mother as the biological dad. An alleged father is also entitled to notice of an adoption, but his rights aren't as strong as those of a presumed father—he doesn't have any greater claim to parentage than the adoptive parents do, and if he receives notice and doesn't file a paternity action within 30 days, his rights can immediately be terminated. A presumed father, on the other hand, has a presumptive right to custody of the child and can prevent the adoption if he does not consent, unless the birth mother can show he's not the biological father, in which case the adoption can proceed without his consent.

Of course, if either a presumed or an alleged father receives notice of the adoption and takes no action, the court can terminate the father's rights and allow the adoption to proceed.

Many states permit minor parents to place a child for adoption, although some require an adult to be involved in the process in some way.

 RESOURCE

State laws on minors' consent to adoption. For details on relevant laws in your state, see www.guttmacher.org (search "minors' rights as parents").

Most states require that a child 12 or older consent to adoption.

Other relatives—for example, the child's grandparents—don't need to consent, and in general aren't even entitled to receive notice of the adoption. A birth mother's parents don't have any legal right to stop her from placing the baby for adoption, and grandparents aren't necessarily favored as adoptive parents over nonrelatives. The only big exception to this rule is the adoption of Native American children, where a special federal law, the Indian Child Welfare Act, applies and does favor adoption by Native American relatives.

If Birth Parents Change Their Minds

Although it's very common to make arrangements for a child to be placed with adoptive parents well before the due date, birth parents cannot give their legal consent to an adoption until after the child is born, and some states require them to wait three to four days after the birth before signing a consent form as part of the adoption process. The consent form is signed during the counseling procedure that birth parents must undergo, whether they're involved in a private agency adoption or an adoption being investigated by a county or state agency.

Until they give written consent, birth parents can legally change their minds about the adoption. Even after the birth parents have given their consent and the child is living in an adoptive home, the birth parents may have some time in which to change their minds and take the child back. In some states, birth parents have as long as three months to revoke their consent—a nerve-wracking time period for the adoptive parents caring for the child.

To help make sure birth parents understand the permanence of adoption and have considered their decision carefully and won't want to change their minds later, some states (and many adoption agencies) require birth parents to undergo counseling before giving consent. In general, the adopting parents pay for the counseling just as they pay most of the expenses of the adoption. See the adoption resources below for information on state consent rules.

Adoption Without Parental Consent

Under a few circumstances, it is possible to go forward with an adoption without a biological parent's consent. If a court terminates parental rights because of abuse, neglect, or abandonment, then the child is free for adoption. Most states' laws provide for termination of parental rights when a parent has willfully failed to support the child or has abandoned the child for a certain period, usually a year. Parental rights can also be terminated if a parent is considered permanently unfit because of drug addiction or child abuse or neglect. If a parent isn't capable of raising a child now but might be later—for example, after alcoholism treatment—the court would more likely order the child placed with a temporary guardian.

Parental rights can be terminated through proceedings in dependency or juvenile court, generally when the child has been removed from the home by an agency such as Child Protective Services. Often, these children are placed with prospective adoptive parents through a foster-adopt program under which the parents are licensed as foster parents with the intention of adopting the child if reunification efforts aren't successful. It's also not uncommon for parental rights to be terminated in the process of a private or agency adoption, in which case the adopting parents would ask the court directly to end the parental rights of an absent father, for example.

Ways to Adopt

Adoptive families come together in different ways. There are public agencies and private agencies, and most counties offer adoption programs as well as foster-adopt procedures. You can also make an arrangement to adopt without using an agency at all. Each option has its good and bad points, so if you're considering adoption make sure you evaluate what's best for you.

Agency Adoptions

A public agency or a private adoption agency licensed by the state can place a child with adoptive parents.

Public agencies generally place children who have become wards of the state because they were orphaned, abandoned, or abused. Many of these children have been in foster care before being freed for adoption. Most public agencies have many children ready to be adopted, many of whom are older or special needs children. Their adoption services are usually free or extremely low cost to the adopting parents, meaning the costs would be limited to incidental expenses.

Open Adoption

An open adoption is one in which there is some degree of contact between the birth parents and adoptive parents both before and after the adoption. There is no one standard for open adoptions. Some adoptive parents meet the birth parents just once before the birth of the child and then don't have much contact afterwards, while others form ongoing relationships that may include written correspondence or visits. Although these visitation agreements are often part of the legal proceedings for the adoption, they are not enforceable by a court. If the adoptive parents don't allow contact after promising to do so, there's not much the birth parents can do.

If you are thinking about using an agency and want your adoption to be open, be sure to check the policies on open placements of any agency you're considering.

RESOURCE

More on open adoptions. The Independent Adoption Center (www.adoptionhelp.org, phone 800-877-OPEN (6736)), is a national nonprofit organization that specializes in open adoptions.

Private agencies are sometimes run by charities or nonprofit social service organizations, but many are for-profit as well. Private agencies specialize in matching would-be adoptive parents with expectant birth parents who want to choose the placement for their baby before the baby is born. The birth parents choose the adoptive parents from a collection of profiles prepared by the prospective parents with the help of the agency.

International adoptions are private agency adoptions, but differ from domestic adoptions in that the children being adopted are usually older, and the match is made by the agency rather than by the birth parents.

Pros and Cons of Private Agency Adoptions

Using a private agency for an adoption offers many advantages:

Experience and expertise. Agencies exist to find children, match them with parents, and satisfy the legal requirements of adoption. They do most of the legwork of an adoption and walk adoptive parents through the steps, such as going through the home study, obtaining the necessary consents, learning the state's legal requirements, and finalizing the papers (often with the help of an attorney).

Extensive counseling throughout the process. Agencies typically provide counseling for adoptive parents, birth parents, and the children (if they are old enough). Careful counseling can help everyone involved weather the emotional ups and downs of the adoption process. Preadoption counseling for a birth mother can help determine whether or not she is really committed to giving up a child for adoption, which reduces the likelihood that she might change her mind.

Specialization. Agencies tend to develop specialties in placing different kinds of children. That can be helpful if you want, for example, to adopt an infant, a child of a different race, a child from another country, or a child with special medical needs.

There are also drawbacks to working with a private agency:

Extreme selectivity choosing adoptive parents. Because private agencies often have a surplus of people who want to adopt, most have long waiting lists of prospective parents, especially for healthy white infants. Agencies sometimes discourage prospective parents from attempting to adopt if the agency believes they bring less than desirable criteria, such as marital status, income, health, religion, family size, and personal history. Many agencies prefer heterosexual married couples. However, for-profit agencies that advertise to the public must comply with state nondiscrimination laws, and can't refuse to do business with prospective parents for a discriminatory reason. The bottom line, of course, comes down to the birth parents, who will use their own criteria to select the adoptive parents with whom they'll place their child.

Lengthy adoption process. As is true in most types of adoption, with an agency adoption, the birth parents must consent to the adoption after the baby is born, and they have a period of time during which they can revoke their consent. In most cases, the agency will place the baby with the prospective adoptive parents anyway, on the assumption that the birth parents won't withdraw consent and that the adoption can be finalized in court after the consent becomes final. If the birth mother decides she wants the child back before the waiting period has expired, the adoptive parents must let the child go. For this reason, agencies sometimes wait to place a child in the adoptive home until all necessary consents have become final, which can be as long as three months in some states. As a result, a child may be placed in foster care for a few days or weeks, depending on the situation and the state's law. This delay concerns many birth and adoptive parents who want the child to have a secure, stable home as soon as possible.

Cost. Adoptive parents can expect to pay a fee of $15,000 or more to adopt a newborn through a private agency, less for placing older or special-needs children. Many agencies charge a flat fee; some use a sliding scale that varies with adoptive parents' income, usually with a minimum and maximum fee. Adoptive parents usually also pay for the birth mother's expenses (medical costs, living expenses during the pregnancy, and costs of counseling) as limited by state law. (See "Payments to Birth Mothers," below.)

TIP

Adoptive parents may get a tax credit. Many of the expenses that adoptive parents incur to legally adopt a child qualify for a federal adoption tax credit. The credit applies to both domestic and international adoptions. (See Chapter 6.)

How to Find and Screen an Adoption Agency

There are thousands of adoption agencies, public and private, in the United States. You'll need to do some searching to find an agency that meets your needs and is able to work with you. Often, a personal referral from someone who has adopted a child is the best way to find a good agency. You can also contact a national adoption organization that offers referrals (some are listed at the end of this chapter).

Once you've got some names, get information from your state's licensing department (search "adoption licensing agency" on your state website). It can tell you whether a particular agency has been cited for licensing violations and whether the licensing office has received any complaints about it. The staff at your state's department of social services may also be able to give you information about the agency.

After you've done your homework, ask each agency about:

- its application process and eligibility requirements (parents' age, health, income, residence, and the like)
- the number of children available for placement by age and other characteristics, and how long a wait the parents might expect
- procedure and timeline for home study
- counseling services (before and after adoption, for birth parents and adoptive parents)
- fees
- accreditation, and

- policies on open adoptions, international adoptions, interstate adoptions, and anything else that's important to you.

Payments to Birth Mothers

It is, of course, illegal to buy or sell a baby. But all states allow adoptive parents to pay a birth mother to cover certain reasonable costs that are specifically related to the adoption process. Most states allow adoptive parents to pay the birth mother's medical expenses, counseling costs, and attorneys' fees. Some states allow payments to cover the birth mother's living expenses, such as food, housing, and transportation, during pregnancy. Most states require all payments to be itemized and approved by a court before the adoption is finalized. Be sure you know and understand your state's laws, because providing or accepting prohibited financial support may jeopardize the adoption—and subject you to criminal charges.

Birth parents who revoke their consent within the time allowed are not legally required to return any of the money they received for expenses during the pregnancy.

A federal adoption tax credit is available for expenses incurred to legally adopt a child. See "Tax Breaks for Adoptive Parents" in Chapter 6 for details.

Independent Adoptions

In an independent or private adoption, a child is placed with adoptive parents without the assistance of an agency. Independent adoptions are arranged directly between the birth parents and the adoptive parents, without the intervention of an agency to make the match. Sometimes, birth parents and adoptive parents meet through personal contacts; other independent adoptions are established through an intermediary such as a lawyer, adoption facilitator, doctor, or member of the clergy. (In some states, adoption facilitators aren't allowed to match adoptive couples with birth parents; in others, it's legal to do so.) Some states allow prospective adoptive parents to advertise in order to meet birth parents, but this isn't legal everywhere.

Regardless of how the match is made, adoptive parents in an independent adoption should have an attorney working with them throughout the process. Independent adoptions are quite heavily regulated, and the legal rules and paperwork are more than most adoptive parents will want to handle themselves—counseling before placement, a significant amount of paperwork required by the local county or state department that investigates the adoption petition, and legal paperwork to finalize the adoption in court.

Independent adoptions are attractive to many birth and adoptive parents for several reasons:

- **Control over the entire adoption process.** Rather than relying on an agency as a go-between, the birth parents and adoptive parents can meet, get to know each other, and decide for themselves whether the adoption should take place and what kind of ongoing communication they would like.

- **Better information.** Adoptive parents can often get background information and medical history on the child and birth family.
- **Less red tape.** Independent adoptions avoid the long waiting lists and restrictive qualifying criteria that characterize many agency adoptions. Independent adoptions can happen much faster than agency adoptions, often within a year of beginning the search for a child. (An agency adoption would take the same amount of time after placement, but the placement process can be lengthy and emotionally draining.)

There are also a few major drawbacks to independent adoptions:

Cost. Because each situation is unique, the expense of an independent adoption is unpredictable. If they advertise or use an adoption facilitator or attorney for the matching process, prospective adoptive parents must cover the cost of finding a birth mother. Even if they meet the birth mother without an intermediary, they'll still pay all costs related to the pregnancy and birth and significant legal fees. Expenses can be higher if the birth mother lives out of state. Some states also allow adoptive parents to pay the birth mother's living expenses during the pregnancy, although there are caps on all of these payments. (See "Payments to Birth Mothers," above.)

Risk. Independent adoptions carry the same risk as agency adoptions, that the birth parents will have a change of heart and withdraw consent during the period before the consent becomes final. In some states, that period is longer in an independent adoption. There's also the possibility that the birth parents won't get adequate preadoption counseling; if they don't fully work through the emotional aspects of giving up a child, it can make an adoption arrangement between birth and adoptive parents more vulnerable to unraveling.

Amount of work. Even with a lawyer's help, many adoptive parents spend enormous amounts of time and money finding a birth mother, not to mention following through and finalizing the adoption, especially if the birth parent lives in another state.

RESOURCE

Resource on independent adoptions. The Independent Adoption Center, www.adoptionhelp.org, is a national nonprofit that specializes in independent adoptions.

Interstate Adoptions

The Interstate Compact on the Placement of Children (ICPC) governs adoptions in which a child is transported across state lines for an adoption. This occurs fairly often with both agency and independent adoptions, and the ICPC is designed to make sure that the adoption is properly investigated by regulating which state is responsible for the home study and what information must change hands during the process. Each state must approve the adoption before it can be finalized.

Identified Adoptions

An identified, or designated, adoption is one in which the adopting parents locate a birth mother (or the other way around) and then ask a private agency to handle the adoption process. In this way, an identified adoption is a hybrid of an independent and an agency adoption. Prospective parents don't have to sit on an agency waiting list, but they reap the other benefits of working with an agency, such as experience with legal issues and counseling services. Identified adoptions provide an alternative to parents in states that don't allow independent adoptions.

Foster Care to Adoption (Fost-Adopt)

Children in foster care are wards of the state, often because they have suffered abuse or neglect or been abandoned by their birth parents. A foster parent is a temporary guardian of a child and is paid monthly support for the child's care. To become a foster parent, your home must be licensed by a state-approved agency. Being a foster parent is very different from becoming a child's guardian, which usually involves a child you already know and doesn't require the same level of screening. (See "Guardianship," below.)

Foster placements can last anywhere from days to years, during which time the parents are entitled to reunification services, which may include substance abuse treatment, anger management training, and education on parenting skills. During this period, the foster parents must cooperate with the reunification plan, even if their hope is to adopt the child. If reunification efforts are unsuccessful, the birth parents' legal rights will be terminated in court, and the child may be placed for adoption, either with the foster parents or another family.

RESOURCE

Resource for foster parents. The National Foster Parent Association (www.nfpaonline.org) is a national support organization for foster parents that provides contact information for state and local associations and other foster care resources.

Stepparent Adoptions

The majority of adoptions in the United States are stepparent adoptions, in which the spouse of a parent adopts that parent's legal child. This type of adoption may occur when one biological parent has died or has left the family after a divorce, and the remaining parent remarries. Most stepparents do not formally adopt their stepchildren, but those who do obtain the same parental rights and responsibilities as biological parents, such as the right to custody and the obligation to pay child support after a divorce.

A stepparent adoption is usually much easier to complete than a nonrelative adoption. The general procedure is the same, but waiting periods are often dispensed with, the home study is fairly minimal, and the cost is significantly less than other types of adoption. After all, the child is already living in the prospective parent's home.

In all stepparent adoptions, however, if the child already has two legal parents, the other one will need to consent. Without consent, the adoption will not be allowed unless the legal parent's parental rights are terminated for some other reason, such as abandonment, unfitness, or failure to support the child. (See "Who Must Consent," above.)

Kinship Adoptions

When a child is related to the adoptive parent by blood or marriage, the adoption is a relative adoption, sometimes called a "kinship adoption." The most common example is a stepparent adoption, but it's also not unusual for grandparents to adopt grandchildren or for aunts and uncles to take responsibility for the children of their siblings if the parents die while the children are minors or if the parents are unable to take care of the children for other reasons. These adoptions are simpler than nonrelative adoptions. If the adopted child has siblings who are not adopted at the same time, kinship adoption procedures usually provide for contact among the siblings after the adoption.

Investigating Adoptive Parents: The Home Study

All states require adoptive parents to undergo an investigation, called a home study, to make sure that they are fit to raise the child they are seeking to adopt. With agency adoptions, parents often undergo a "preplacement" investigation that verifies they are appropriate adoptive parents. But in addition, all adoptive parents must go through a full investigation once a child is placed with them for adoption. (If there was a preplacement home study, then the second investigation is called "postplacement.")

Who conducts the home study depends on what type of adoption is involved. In an independent or stepparent adoption, a county or state agency is responsible for the investigation. When an agency does the placement, the same agency also does the home study. The home study process involves a licensed social worker employed by the county, state, or agency who interviews the adoptive parents, examines their home life, and collects other information from personal references and background checks. The investigating social worker gets information about issues such as the prospective adoptive parents' financial situation, employment history, marital and family history, other children (current or planned), work and career obligations, physical and mental health, and criminal history.

The social worker also gathers information from a number of personal references, verifies employment, and requires the prospective adoptive parents to be fingerprinted and checked against national criminal databases. Finally, the social worker must check into whether there's anyone else with a right to object to the adoption. If the child being adopted has a birth father who hasn't consented, for example, the social worker will explore the situation with the birth mother and encourage the adoptive parents to have his rights terminated before the final hearing. The social worker will include in the report whether there are any other involved parties and whether any additional consents are needed.

In recent years, the home study has become more than just a method of investigating prospective parents; it serves to educate and inform them as well. The social worker helps to prepare the adoptive parents by discussing issues such as how and when to talk with the child about being adopted, how to deal with the reactions of friends and family to the adoption, communicating with the birth parents in an open adoption, and other issues.

The home study typically takes several months. Once all of the information has been gathered, the social worker submits a report for the court with a recommendation about whether or not the particular adoption should be approved.

It doesn't happen very often, but if the social worker writes a negative report to the court, the prospective adoptive parents may contest the conclusion. Each state has different appeal procedures. Some states provide for a separate procedure, while other states make the appeal part of the adoption hearing.

Prospective adoptive parents may be charged a fee for a home study. It depends on the type of adoption and agency involved; there may be no fee with a public agency or a few thousand dollars' fee with a private agency.

Family Court Approval of Adoption

All adoptions, whether handled by an agency or done independently, must be approved by a local court—often the family court, but sometimes the probate department or the general civil court. The adoptive parents file an adoption petition when the child is first placed with them. In most cases, the home study is conducted after the petition is filed; once it's complete, the social worker files the report with the court and the judge holds a hearing. Even the simplest stepparent adoption requires a hearing, in which the adoptive parents and the child appear before the judge and confirm their commitment to the adoption.

Giving Notice to Interested Parties

In general, all of the consents will be taken care of during the investigation process. If there is anyone whose consent is necessary and who has refused to consent, that person—usually a birth father—must be given notice of the adoption hearing and the right to appear and contest the adoption. If that person does show up at the hearing, the judge will have to decide whether to consider the arguments against the adoption at that time or postpone the hearing until everyone has had a chance to prepare for a contested trial. Most of the time, however, all of this will have been dealt with during the investigation process.

The Adoption Petition

An adoption petition generally includes:
- the names and address of the adoptive parents
- the name, age, and legal parentage of the child to be adopted
- the relationship between the adoptive parents and the child to be adopted, such as blood relative, stepparent, or nonrelative
- the legal reason that the birth parents' rights are being terminated (usually, because they consent)
- an assertion that the adoptive parents are the appropriate people to adopt the child, and
- an assertion that the adoption is in the child's best interest.

Sometimes, the written consent of the birth parents or a court order terminating their parental rights is filed along with the petition. Other times, the termination occurs later in the process. Adoptive parents also often include a request to have the child's name legally changed. If the child's name is not changed as part of the adoption, and the adopting parents later want to change it, they'll need to file a separate court proceeding.

Adoption Hearing and Order

When it's time for the adoption hearing, the judge will have a chance to review the home study report in advance. The adoptive parents and the child must appear in court and, in most cases, the judge will ask them some simple questions—usually just verifying that the facts in the petition are true, and that the parents are committed to the adoption. If the child is older, the judge may also ask the child some questions. Some judges make adoption hearings quite informal and hold them in chambers (the judge's office), and others do them in open court with a court reporter present. Either way, adoption hearings are private, and the public isn't allowed. However, most judges will allow you to bring other family members and friends to the hearing if you wish.

If the judge determines that the adoption is in the child's best interest, the judge will issue an order approving and finalizing the adoption. This order, often called a final decree of adoption, legalizes the new parent-child relationship, orders a name change if the new parents have asked for one, and is the final step in the adoption. Finalizing an adoption is one of the happiest things that ever happens in a courtroom.

RESOURCE

Helpful resources on adoptions:

- www.adoption.com. This website provides information about adoption agencies, international adoption, and many other adoption issues, including links to a wide variety of state adoption laws, such as consent to adoption, regulation of adoption expenses, use of advertising in adoption, access to adoption records, and more.

- www.childwelfare.gov/adoption. The Child Welfare Information Gateway, a program of the U.S. Department of Health & Human Services, provides information about adoption and referrals to state and local agencies and support groups. The site also includes the National Foster Care & Adoption Directory (see www.childwelfare.gov/nfcad), which lists public and licensed private adoption agencies in the United States as well as adoption support groups.

- www.nacac.org. The North American Council on Adoptable Children provides extensive adoption resources, from adoption agencies to post-adoption support groups.

Adult Adoptions

In most states, it's legal for one adult to adopt another as long as there's at least a ten-year age difference and the parties can show why the adoption is in the interests of both people and the public good. Often, adult adoptions are stepparent adoptions that the family didn't get around to when the younger person was a minor, but wants to complete now so the younger person will inherit from the older.

Sometimes, older adults who don't have children of their own meet younger persons whom they wish to treat as their children for inheritance purposes. Although adult adoptions can generally be completed based on the two adults' agreement, without a home study or investigation, many states require investigations of adult adoptions where caregivers of the elderly are involved, in order to prevent older people from being manipulated or abused.

International Adoptions

Adopting a child from another country is complicated, not least because the rules depend on whether the country has adopted the Hague Convention and whether the child is an orphan. In addition to satisfying the adoption requirements of both the child's country and the parents' home state in the United States, parents must get an immigrant visa for the child through U.S. Citizenship and Immigration Services (USCIS) and the State Department. The adoptive parents of orphans must be married and at least 21 years old or, if single, at least 25 years old. In most cases, the child must be under 16 years of age when the parents file the initial immigration petition. USCIS also requires adoptive parents to complete several forms and submit a favorable home study report from a licensed agency.

The country from which you're adopting is likely to have its own requirements as well—many have both a minimum and a maximum age for adoptive parents, many require that adoptive parents be married, and most discourage or prohibit same-sex couples or out LGBT people.

Most people go through an American agency that specializes in international adoptions. You can adopt directly, but it's less common, because the rules are so complicated. In general, the agency you choose will help you select a country to work with and help match you with a child. You can either wait to file your adoption petition until you've been matched with an identified child, or file a petition in advance to get things started.

Finally, be sure to check your own state laws for any preadoption requirements. Some states, for instance, require you to submit the written consent of the birth mother before they approve the entry of the child into the state.

Parents who adopt overseas may need to readopt the child in their own state in order to make sure that the adoption fully conforms to state law. Sometimes, readoption is a legal necessity—required either by the state in which you live or by the country in which you adopted. Doing so also has the advantage of allowing you to obtain a birth certificate in English, which you often will not have when you leave the host country.

RESOURCE

More on international adoptions:

- The U.S. State Department, http://adoption.state.gov, and the U.S. Citizenship and Immigration Services, www.uscis. gov (click on "Adoption" or call 800-375-5283) provide information and forms related to international adoption.
- *U.S. Immigration Made Easy,* by Ilona Bray (Nolo), discusses the rules and application procedures for international adoptions and citizenship for adopted children. See www. nolo.com for a sample chapter and full table of contents.

Same-Sex Couples and Adoption

Given the confusing and quickly changing status of same-sex marriage and marriage-like relationships (domestic partnerships and civil unions), it's not surprising that the laws surrounding the children born or adopted into same-sex relationships are also in flux.

Second-Parent Adoption

When one person in a same-sex couple has a child—by adopting, giving birth, or, in the case of a gay man using a surrogate to carry a child conceived with his sperm and a donor egg—the other partner generally has no biological relationship to the child. In most states, that person has no legal relationship to the child, either, and to become the child's legal parent, the partner must adopt the child through a second parent or coparent adoption. (The exception is in states with marriage or marriage equivalent laws, discussed in Chapter 1, where a married person is a legal parent of a child born into the legal partnership. However, adoptions are still recommended in those cases, to protect the second parent's rights in other states and where federal law is involved.)

There are more than 20 states where laws are in place allowing second-parent adoption. In other states, there's no specific law, but many courts will allow the adoptions. However, some states—including Kentucky, Nebraska, North Carolina, and Ohio—have expressly disapproved of this type of adoption.

Adopting Together

Many same-sex couples have happily adopted children together. But there's no denying that same-sex couples who seek to adopt may face obstacles at several steps along the way. Some adoption agencies don't accept same-sex couples, or at least actively discourage them from seeking to adopt. Some birth parents won't choose them. Some judges might refuse to approve them as adoptive parents. However, at least 21 states have expressly ruled that a gay couple may adopt a child together when neither is the child's legal parent, and such adoptions have been granted in a number of other states as well.

RESOURCE

Resources on same-sex couples and adoption:
The Human Rights Campaign website (www.hrc.org) includes information on state adoption laws affecting LGBT individuals and same-sex couples. Also, the National Center for Lesbian Rights (www.nclrights.org), Lambda Legal (www.lambdalegal.org), and Gay & Lesbian Advocates & Defenders (www.glaad.org) all offer information and resources.

Working With a Lawyer

Although there is no legal requirement that a lawyer be involved in an adoption, the process can be complex, and many adopting families seek out someone with experience and expertise. This is especially true when parents pursue an independent adoption and don't go through an agency. Even adoptive parents who work with an agency, however, often hire a lawyer to prepare the adoption petition and represent them at the hearing. Many stepparents, however, represent themselves, as the process is quite simple in most places.

Adopted Children's Right to Their Birth Records

After an adoption is completed, the state where the child was born will issue a new birth certificate showing the adoptive parents as the child's parents. The original birth certificate, showing the birth parents, is sealed so that no one can see it without court permission. Only a few states offer adult adopted children open access to their original birth certificates. Generally, a court will unseal a record only for an urgent reason, such as a need for medical or genetic information.

But as attitudes toward adoption have become more open, states have come up with ways for adopted children to find their birth parents, some of which do not require the unsealing of records. One system is called "search and consent." Someone who was adopted as a child contacts the birth parent through an intermediary agency; if the birth parent agrees, the agency gives the contact information to the child. This only works when the birth parent's information is available, and the most common system is a mutual consent registry, used in about 25 states, in which birth parents and adopted children provide identifying information about themselves to the registry. If a birth parent and that parent's adopted child both appear within a registry, the agency in charge shares the information with each of them, allowing them to get in touch.

> ⊙ **TIP**
>
> **Let an agency help you.** If you're searching for a birth parent, contact a local adoption agency that is familiar with states' laws and procedures for contacting birth parents. The resources listed above, such as www.adoption.com, often provide referrals to local agencies.

Guardianship

A guardianship is a legal arrangement in which an adult has the court-ordered authority and responsibility to care for a child. A guardianship may be necessary if a child's parents die or if the child has been abandoned, neglected, or abused. Guardianships usually involve people who know each other or are related, in contrast to foster care situations, where a family is licensed to provide foster care in its home and then takes in whatever child is in need of care. A guardian does not have to be licensed in advance by the state, but before a formal legal guardianship will be granted, the county does investigate the request.

Typically, a guardian takes care of a child's personal needs, including shelter, education, and medical care. A guardian may also provide financial management for a child, though sometimes a second person (often called a "guardian of the estate") is appointed to manage the child's assets.

A guardianship does not sever the legal relationship (regarding custody, support, and inheritance) between the biological parents and the child the way an adoption does. For example, if a biological parent dies without a will, the child who is under a guardianship may inherit under state law. A child who has been adopted generally does not inherit from a biological parent who dies without a will.

As a general rule, guardianships are not granted unless the parents consent, the parents have abandoned the child, or a judge finds that it would be detrimental to the child for the parents to have custody.

If the court decides parents are unfit, a guardian will be appointed even if they object. The person who wants to be the guardian begins the process (generally, but not always, with a lawyer's help) by filing papers in court. A court investigator will interview the prospective guardian, the child, and the child's parents and make a recommendation to the judge. A judge will review the case, including any objections from family members to the proposed guardian, and decide who, if anyone, should be appointed guardian.

A guardianship ordinarily lasts until the child becomes a legal adult (age 18 in most cases); the child dies; the child's assets are used up—if the guardianship was set up solely for the purpose of handling the child's finances; or a judge determines that a guardianship is no longer necessary.

A guardian may step down from the role only with permission from the court. In that case, a judge will appoint a replacement guardian.

Alternatives to Legal Guardianship

Some adults raise children—often grandchildren or other relatives—without legal court authorization. There are simple forms that parents can use to authorize other adults to care for their children in many circumstances, and those work fine for a short-term care situation. (For example, California has a form called a Caregiver's Authorization Affidavit, which gives a nonparent permission to enroll a child in school and make medical decisions on the child's behalf without going to court; other states have similar forms.) However, if the caretaking role is going to last longer than a couple of months, it's best to get a legal guardianship—otherwise you could run into problems with institutions that won't accept your authority to make decisions for the child.

Research the laws for your state or talk to a knowledge-able family law attorney to find out whether there are ways for you to take legal responsibility for a child—short of becoming a legal guardian.

Children

Many local, state, and federal laws are designed to protect children, whether it's prohibiting them from drinking alcohol or working long hours, or requiring them to go to school. There are special juvenile courts to handle kids who get in trouble, with an emphasis on rehabilitation rather than punishment. Kids even help their parents qualify for tax breaks—but may also cost them if the kids cause damage, because parents are held responsible for many of their children's actions.

Baby's First Legal Documents

A birth certificate and Social Security card are the first two legal documents a child needs.

Birth Certificate

A birth certificate serves as proof of your baby's name, date of birth, citizenship, and parentage. You will need a copy of the birth certificate when enrolling your child in school, applying for a passport for your child, and at other important points in your child's life.

The birth certificate process begins with a birth registration form, which new parents are given before a newborn baby is discharged from the hospital. The form asks for the parents' names and Social Security numbers, the child's date of birth, and the child's name. If parents complete the form in the hospital, the staff will submit it to the state department in charge of issuing birth certificates, often called the department of vital statistics.

If the baby isn't born in a medical facility, the mother or the physician or midwife assisting in the delivery must notify health officials of the birth. If you're planning a home birth, you can contact your state's department of health or bureau of vital statistics for more information. Your doctor or midwife should be familiar with the procedures as well.

When parents are not married, the father must sign a voluntary acknowledgment of paternity to be named as the child's father on the birth certificate. The "Unmarried Parents" section of Chapter 4 covers paternity.

Most issuing agencies—either the state or the local county registrar—will automatically send new parents a copy of the birth certificate once it's issued; in other states, parents have to make a formal request to the appropriate department and pay a small fee. You can always get additional copies of your child's birth certificate from your county registrar or from the state bureau of vital statistics.

Naming Your Baby

In most states, you may give your child any first, middle, and last name you like. Whether you are married or not, you don't have to give your baby the last name of either parent if you don't want to, and the child does not have to have the father's last name to be considered his legal child.

Social Security Number

Your child will need a Social Security number. You will need the number to add your new baby to your health insurance plan, set up a college savings plan or bank account for your child, or apply for government benefits that could help your child and family. It's also required if you want to claim child-related tax breaks (discussed below) on your income taxes.

The easiest way to apply for a Social Security number for your child is through the same birth registration form that you used to get your child's birth certificate. The birth registration form has a box you can check to request a Social Security number for your child. To complete the form, you will need to provide both parents' Social Security numbers.

If you didn't get a birth registration form in the hospital, you can visit your local Social Security Administration (SSA) office and request a number in person. This process requires you to do three things:

- Complete Form SS-5 (*Application for a Social Security Number*) and provide both parents' Social Security numbers on the form. To save time, download Form SS-5 from the SSA website (www.ssa.gov/online/ss-5. pdf) and complete it before you go.
- Provide at least two documents proving your baby's age, identity, and citizenship status. One document should be your child's birth certificate. The other document can be your child's hospital birth record or other medical record.

- Provide proof of your own identity. Your driver's license and passport are both acceptable.

Social Security Numbers for Adopted Children

If you adopt a child who is a U.S. citizen, your child probably has a Social Security number already. If not, you can obtain an Adoption Taxpayer Identification Number (ATIN) to claim child-related tax breaks while the adoption is pending. To apply for one, complete IRS Form W-7A, *Application for Taxpayer Identification Number for Pending U.S. Adoptions*, available at www.irs.gov. The ATIN will be valid for two years, at which point you can extend it if your child's adoption is still not final. Once the adoption is final, you must stop using the ATIN and get a Social Security number for your child following the process described above.

If you are adopting a child from another country, you will have to wait until the adoption is final and your child has entered the United States before you can obtain a Social Security number for your child. Once that happens, you can use the process described above.

Find the SSA office nearest you by logging on to the SSA's Office Locator at www.ssa.gov/locator. If you'd prefer, you can mail in a completed Form SS-5 along with your identification documents to your local SSA office. To find yours, call the SSA at 800-772-1213. Most people apply in person, however, because you'll need to give the SSA originals or certified copies of all identification documents, and going in person means you don't let those important documents out of your hands (or spend money getting additional certified copies).

Once you've submitted your application, you should receive your child's Social Security card in six to 12 weeks. It may take substantially longer to process your application if your child is one year of age or older, because the SSA will contact your state's department of vital statistics to confirm that the birth certificate you have provided is valid.

Is Your Child a U.S. Citizen?

Every baby born in the United States is an American citizen, regardless of the parents' citizenship. In other words, a new baby is a citizen even if the parents are resident aliens or undocumented immigrants. All that is required is that your baby be born on U.S. soil. (There is one exception to this rule for certain children of diplomatic personnel, but it does not apply to the vast majority of people who live in the United States.)

There is no special paperwork to complete to establish your child's citizenship status—the child's birth certificate will serve as proof of citizenship. If you do not reside in the U.S. legally, then your U.S. citizen child may someday be able to petition for you to receive lawful permanent residency (a green card)—but only after the child turns 21. And you have no legal right to live in the United States until then, unless you are able to maintain a separate, valid visa (which is unlikely). If you somehow managed to stay in the United States without documentation all that time, current immigration laws would punish you by mandating a ten-year exile from the United States before being allowed back in after the consular interview at which you would apply for your green card. See a lawyer for an analysis of your personal situation.

Citizenship rules are much more complex for children born outside of the United States to at least one U.S. citizen parent. If one or both parents are U.S. citizens and married at the time the child is born, a child born after 1986 is considered a U.S. citizen provided that at least one U.S. citizen parent actually lived in the United States at some point before the child was born. Different (and more complicated) requirements apply if the parents are not married. To find out whether your foreign-born child meets the standards for citizenship, contact your local U.S. consular office. If your foreign-born child qualifies for citizenship, you will need to register the birth with your local U.S. consular office and obtain a *Consular Report of Birth Abroad of a Citizen of the United States of America* (FS-240). You can find contact information for your local consular office at www.usembassy.gov. To learn more about citizenship rules for children born abroad, log on to http://travel.state.gov/content/passports/english/abroad/events-and-records/birth.html.

If you are a U.S. citizen and adopt a foreign-born child, either from overseas or from within the United States, that child will, in most cases, become a citizen automatically. The timing, however, as well as the way you'd obtain a certificate proving citizenship, depend on various factors. Ask the adoption agency or lawyer assisting you to analyze the details in your case. For more information on adoption, see Chapter 5.

Tax Breaks for Parents

The federal government offers parents several money-saving tax breaks to ease the financial burden of caring for children.

Dependent Exemption

The dependent exemption allows qualified parents to deduct a certain amount—$3,950 per child in 2014—from their taxable income. With some exceptions, parents can claim this exemption for any child who:

- is your biological, step-, adopted, or foster child
- lived with you for more than half the year
- is younger than 19 at the end of the tax year, is a full-time student younger than 24, or is permanently and totally disabled, and
- didn't provide more than half of his or her own support for the year.

For 2014, the dependent exemption is subject to phaseout if your income exceeds certain income levels. The phaseout applies once adjusted gross income (AGI) exceeds $254,200 (single), $305,050 (married filing jointly), $279,650 (head of household), and $152,525 (married filing separately). For each $2,500 of AGI over the threshold, dependent exemptions are reduced by 2%. This phaseout did not apply for tax years 2010 through 2012 but was reinstated for 2013.

When parents are divorced, a child is the dependent of the parent who has physical custody, because the child lives with that parent for more than half the year. (Parents who share physical custody equally often designate one of them as having 51% custody in order to allow that person to take the exemption.) Divorced parents can also agree that the noncustodial parent take the dependent exemption for the child; the custodial parent must sign a form transferring the exemption to the other parent. See Chapter 4 for more on the subject of the dependent exemption and child support.

RESOURCE

More about the dependent exemption. See IRS Publication 501, *Exemptions, Standard Deduction, and Filing Information,* available at www.irs.gov.

Child Tax Credit

The child tax credit allows qualified parents to subtract $1,000 per child (2014 tax year) from their federal tax bill. The eligibility requirements are essentially the same as those for the dependent exemption, with two notable exceptions: The child must be younger than 17 (rather than 19, as is the case with the dependent exemption), and there's a lower income limit for the child tax credit. For the 2014 tax year, married couples filing jointly cannot claim any part of the child tax credit if their adjusted gross income exceeds $110,000.

If you and your child's other parent are divorced, the custodial parent will take the child tax credit, unless the noncustodial parent is taking the dependent exemption by agreement with the custodial parent. In that case, the noncustodial parent can take the child tax credit as well as the dependent exemption.

> **RESOURCE**
> **More about the child tax credit.** See IRS Publication 972, *Child Tax Credit*, available at www.irs.gov.

Tax Breaks for Adoptive Parents

Through the adoption tax credit, the federal government in essence reimburses adoptive parents for the expenses they incur to legally adopt a child. The credit allows you to subtract your adoption expenses from your tax liability for the year. For tax year 2014, the maximum credit available for qualifying expenses is $13,190 per adoption.

To claim the credit, the following rules apply:

- Your child must be younger than 18 (or, if older than 18, must be incapable of caring for himself or herself because of a disability).
- You must have out-of-pocket costs related to the adoption, such as adoption fees, court costs, attorneys' fees, and travel expenses.
- Your income must be within certain limits. For the 2014 tax year, the credit completely phases out at $237,880.

Expenses of stepparent adoptions or surrogate parenting arrangements do not qualify for the adoption tax credit.

RESOURCE

More about the adoption tax credit. Find out more about income limits, rules for children with special needs, and rules for domestic and international adoptions in IRS Form 8839, *Qualified Adoption Expenses*, available at www.irs.gov.

Child Care Tax Breaks

The federal government offers two tax breaks to help offset the cost of child care: the child care credit and dependent care accounts.

Child Care Credit

The child care credit provides a tax credit of 20% to 35% of the first $3,000 in child care costs you incur per child per year (with a maximum of $6,000 for two or more children). The exact percentage is determined by your income level.

You must meet all of the following requirements (with some exceptions) to be eligible for the child care credit (the same rules apply to dependent care accounts, discussed below):

- Your child must be your biological, adopted, step-, or foster child.
- Your child must live with you for more than half the year.
- Your child must be younger than 13 or permanently and totally disabled.
- You must pay more than half the cost of keeping up a home in which you and your child live during the year.

- You (and your spouse, if you are married) must work, look for work, or be a full-time student.

In addition to the above, your child care expenses must meet all of the following criteria:

- Your child care provider must be someone whom you can't claim as a dependent—this may include a licensed day care provider, preschool, or on-the-books nanny, but can't include anyone you pay under the table.
- You must have used the child care to enable you to work, look for work, or attend school full time (for example, you cannot claim a credit for babysitter costs incurred to run errands or go out on Saturday night).
- Payments to a child care provider must have been for child care only, not for items such as food, lodging, clothing, education, or entertainment for the child care worker. (Expenses for household services, such as housekeeping, qualify if they are at least partly for the well-being and protection of your child.)

Claiming the child care credit is easy. Keep your child care expense receipts for the year and then input the appropriate information onto your tax return.

RESOURCE

More about the child care credit. See IRS Publication 503, *Child and Dependent Care Expenses,* available at www.irs.gov.

Dependent Care Accounts

A dependent care account (sometimes called a dependent care flexible spending account or a cafeteria plan) is like the 401(k) plan of the child care world. Through your employer, you set aside pretax dollars that you can access to pay your nanny, day care, or preschool bills during the year. All of the money you contribute to the account is exempt from federal taxes. Not all employers offer dependent care accounts, and you can't set up an individual account—they're only available through work. Also, if you sign up for a dependent care account, you can't also claim a child care tax credit for the same child care expenses.

Federal law sets limits on the amount you can contribute to your dependent care account. Regardless of how many children you have, married couples filing jointly can contribute a maximum of $5,000. Single people or married couples filing separately can contribute up to $2,500. Your employer can set an amount lower than the federal maximum.

The eligibility rules for a dependent care account are the same as for the child care credit discussed above.

The amount you can use from your dependent care account is limited by your earned income. You cannot claim more than your earned income or your spouse's earned income, whichever is less.

If your employer sponsors a dependent care account, you'll be able to enroll during your general benefits enrollment period. At that point, you decide how much money to contribute for the year (you can't change this amount during the year—and if you don't spend it by the end of the year, you will usually lose it).

To access money from your dependent care account, you must have already incurred the expense—you can't take money out in advance. You'll submit a form and the receipt to your employer, who will reimburse you for the expense directly or through a third-party administrator. Consult your employee benefits manual or check with your human resources administrator for more information on your company's reimbursement policy.

You will also have to include this information on your tax return.

Child Care by the Books

To take advantage of child care tax breaks, you must comply with appropriate laws. For example, if you hire a nanny, you are subject to several federal and state employment laws. These include:

- verifying your caregiver's immigration status
- delivering regular paychecks
- withholding and paying Social Security, Medicare, and other applicable taxes
- getting an employer identification number, and
- paying for workers' compensation insurance.

For detailed legal and practical advice on hiring in-home child care, see *Nannies & Au Pairs: Hiring In-Home Child Care*, by Ilona Bray (Nolo). See www.nolo.com for a sample chapter and full table of contents.

RESOURCE

More about dependent care accounts. See IRS Publication 503, *Child and Dependent Care Expenses* (and IRS Form 2441), available at www.irs.gov.

Keeping Children Safe

Many local, state, and federal laws treat children differently from adults.

Alcohol, Drugs, and Tobacco

Many states have special rules designed to protect children from drinking and drugs.

Alcohol. In every state, the legal drinking age is 21. There are related rules and penalties regarding possession of alcohol, driving under the influence, and carrying or using a fake ID. Parents may be found liable if they serve alcohol to minors and damage ensues—including injuries or damage from a car accident caused by an underage child who was allowed to drink in their home. See the Mothers Against Drunk Driving website (www.madd.org) for extensive information on underage drinking.

Tobacco. State laws prohibit a minor from buying cigarettes or other tobacco products, and require stores to check ID before selling them. See the American Lung Association website (www.lung.org) for links to state rules and articles on smoking by children.

Drugs. Punishments for the possession, use, or sale (or intent to sell) of illicit drugs, such as marijuana, heroin, cocaine, and amphetamines, depend on the substance (marijuana penalties are less severe) and the age of the person. Where the violation occurred also matters; selling or possessing marijuana on school grounds carries more severe penalties. See the National Alliance of State Drug Enforcement Agencies (www.nasdea.org/members.html) for links to state drug enforcement agencies, and the National Organization for the Reform of Marijuana Laws (www.norml.org) for state marijuana laws.

Bikes, Scooters, and Skateboards

Local governments often set rules limiting the places where kids can bike, skateboard, or ride a scooter. Many states require all kids under 18 to wear helmets while bicycling.

Kids in Cars

All states require special child car seats, though the exact rules about their use vary. For instance, some states require car seats for children until they're eight years old, but others end the requirement when kids reach six years old or weigh 60 pounds. In California, kids must ride in the backseat, even when they no longer are required to use a car seat. State laws also prohibit leaving young children alone in a car. Contact your state motor vehicle agency for information on laws that affect minors.

Tattoos and Piercing

Many states prohibit children under age 18 from getting their ears, lips, or other parts of their body pierced without parental consent. Some prohibit tattooing of children under age 18 whether or not the parents consent.

RESOURCE

Tattoo and body piercing rules. See your state rules at the National Conference of State Legislatures' website, www.ncsl. org/research/health/tattooing-and-body-piercing.aspx. Also, check your state department of health.

Online Dangers

The Internet offers children as well as adults many great activities, both educational and fun. But the online world also presents dangers to children, from inappropriate use of kids' personal information to exposure to pornography and sexual predators. Federal and state laws regulate Internet use involving children by controlling things such as what can be sent to a child. The Children's Online Privacy Protection Act (COPPA) limits information that websites can collect from kids under age 13, including information kids post about themselves or personal information such as their addresses or phone numbers. COPPA requires websites to post their privacy policies. Many states are also setting rules against "cyberbullying." (See "Bullying and Harassment," below.)

Ultimately, it is parents who need to supervise their children's computer use and set rules on smart and safe use of the Internet and websites like YouTube and Facebook. See the resources that follow to learn more.

RESOURCE

How to protect your kids online. For detailed advice on Internet safety for children, see www.protectkids.com, a sister site of the national nonprofit Enough Is Enough (www.enough.org). Both sites include tips for both parents and children on safe use of the Internet, including use of monitoring and filtering software. The federal government's website www.onguardonline.gov provides lots of articles on Internet safety. For information on federal privacy rules under the Children's Online Privacy Protection Act (COPPA) go to the Federal Trade Commission website (www.ftc.gov) and search "COPPA." To report unsolicited obscene material sent to a child, contact the National Center for Missing and Exploited Children at www.cybertipline.com or call 800-843-5678.

TIP

How to remove personal information from the Internet (including information your kids have posted online). Make sure your kids know not to post any personal information (such as name, address, and phone number) online. The Privacy Rights Clearinghouse (www.privacyrights.org) has useful advice on the subject of controlling personal information online in the "Online Privacy & Technology" section.

Bullying and Harassment

Bullying, both physical (hitting and punching) and verbal, is an increasing concern of children and families, and many states and local school districts have responded by passing strict antibullying rules and instituting educational programs. Many rules prohibit specific bullying behavior, including harassment based on sexual orientation. Increasingly, schools are required to notify parents when their child is involved in bullying (as either victim or instigator). Depending on the situation, penalties for bullying may include suspension or expulsion from school to charges of felony assault.

"Cyberbullying" occurs when a kid (or group of kids) bullies someone online, via cell phone, or by some other form of technology. Cyberbullying can include sending cruel or threatening emails and posting negative comments, photos, or videos online, whether via instant messaging or on a Facebook page or another social networking site. Although cyberbullying involves the Internet service provider (ISP) as the place where the messages are posted, it's difficult to get an ISP to block such activities. Under the Communications Decency Act, ISPs are immune from liability for such activity and, as a result, have little incentive to cooperate in removing it.

RESOURCE

More about bullying and how to stop it. An excellent website that provides advice for families, children, and schools on how to identify and prevent bullying is www.stopbullying.gov, a special program of the U.S. Department of Health & Human Services. The site also lists states with antibullying laws. Other useful sites with advice for parents and teachers on how to stop bullying are the Gay, Lesbian & Straight Education Network (www.glsen.org) and the Anti-Defamation League (www.adl.org/combatbullying).

Teen Driving

Many states have age-specific rules about driving—for example, when a teen can get a learner's (or instructor's) permit to drive, requirements for a set number of hours of professional driver education training, and mandatory supervised training with an adult. Once a minor gets a license, states may restrict the age and number of passengers who can be in a car with the new driver and the hours a novice driver can be on the road. In California, for example, in a minor's first year driving, the new driver may not drive (with a few exceptions) with anyone under the age of 20 in the car and may not drive between 11 p.m. and 5 a.m. unless accompanied by a driver who is 25 years of age or older. Penalties for drunk driving also vary for young drivers. Rules vary from state to state, so check your state department of motor vehicles for details.

Unfit Parents

Parents who abuse, neglect, or abandon children can be considered unfit. Where the children have another fit parent, the offending parent may lose custody or visitation rights; in other cases the parent can lose parental rights, either permanently or temporarily.

When a parent completely abandons a child—providing no care or financial support—and there's no other adult to care for the child, the state's foster care system will take charge. (If there is a relative available, guardianship is usually a better option.) When a parent is abusive or neglectful or is abusing substances or otherwise failing to care for children appropriately, a relative can step in and care for the child under an informal or formal guardianship, or the child can be placed in foster care while the state attempts to help the parent deal with the issues and reunite with the child. If these efforts aren't successful, the child will usually be freed for adoption. In especially severe cases, parents may be charged with a crime. (For more on foster care and guardianship, see Chapter 5.)

Parents who physically abandon a very young child may be criminally prosecuted. But there are "safe haven" or "legal abandonment" laws in almost every state that designate certain places or people as drop-off locations where a parent can leave an infant without fear of prosecution. These are usually hospitals, fire stations, or with an emergency responder. These laws only apply to very young babies—in some states, the child must be less than 72 hours old, while other states extend the time period all the way to 90 days.

Leaving a Child Home Alone

When does a child have enough maturity and physical, mental, and emotional ability to stay at home alone safely? Many states advise against leaving children younger than 12, but age isn't the only factor. The time of day, length of time the child will be left alone, and the safety of the neighborhood are also major considerations. Depending on your state laws and child protective policies, leaving a young child unsupervised may be considered neglect. For more information, see the *Leaving Your Child Home Alone* fact sheet of the Child Welfare Information Gateway at www. childwelfare.gov/pubs/factsheets/homealone.cfm.

Crimes Against Children

All states make child abuse (physical, sexual, or emotional) a crime and require physicians, teachers, and other professionals with knowledge of child development to report suspected abuse to the police or a child protective services agency. Penalties are severe for someone who abuses a child (or allows abuse by another) and can include lengthy prison terms.

Arguably less serious than child abuse, child endangerment is also a crime. Examples include leaving a child unattended in a car, inflicting physical punishment that results in bodily injury, manufacturing drugs in the presence of a child, or leaving a young child unsupervised in an unsafe area.

RESOURCE

Find your child protective services agency. For immediate help, contact your local police. You can also find the websites and phone numbers of your state's agencies designated to investigate suspected child abuse and neglect at the Child Welfare Information Gateway, www.childwelfare.gov, a service of the Children's Bureau, Administration for Children & Families, U.S. Department of Health & Human Services (phone 800-394-3366). You can also contact the Childhelp National Child Abuse Hotline at 800-4-A-CHILD (or see their website at www.childhelp.org). This hotline offers crisis intervention and referrals to emergency, social service, and support resources. All calls are anonymous and confidential.

Many federal laws protect children from sexual crimes, particularly as concerns child pornography and sexual exploitation. See www.fbi.gov for details.

Age of Consent to Have Sex

Men having sex with girls younger than a specified age has for centuries been known as "statutory rape." The age of consent when the first statutory rape laws were written in 1275 was 12, and that remained largely unchanged until the late nineteenth century, when feminists sought to raise the age of consent in order to end the widespread abuse of working class girls. Then, in the 1970s, a second wave of feminists argued successfully for gender-neutral laws that would also punish older females who had sex with younger males, and the laws now apply in both directions. (However, the need to protect young women from sexual coercion and exploitation was never repudiated.)

Today, there is no nationwide age at which girls are deemed capable of giving consent. Instead, most states vary the age of consent depending on the age differences between the partners, the age of the "victim," or the age of the defendant. For example, one state might make 16 the age of consent, but require an age differential of four years or more before the activity is illegal. Sexual relations between a 17-year-old and a 15-year-old would be legal in such a state, but not relations between the same 15-year-old and someone who's 21. In other states, the age of consent itself may change depending on the age of the perpetrator: In such a state, the normal age of consent (16) will drop to 13 if the perpetrator is no more than four years older and younger than 19. Yet other states specify a minimum age of the perpetrator, making it illegal to have relations with someone below the age of consent only if the perpetrator is over 18 years old.

Most statutory rape laws do not allow perpetrators to argue that they reasonably thought that the victim was over the age of consent.

Medical Care

Until a child is legally an adult, parents have the right to make decisions about their child's medical care and treatment. There are a few important exceptions to this rule, however, designed to protect teenagers who can't rely on parental support. For example, depending upon the state and the age of the child, a minor may be able to make decisions without parental consent when it comes to seeking prenatal care (in the case of a pregnant teen, for example); treatment related to a sexually transmitted infection, drug problem, or rape; or access to birth control. A few states allow minors to consent to abortion services without parental consent, although many states require some kind of parental involvement in a minor's decision to have an abortion, such as the prior notification to or consent of at least one parent. Many states allow minors to place children for adoption.

RESOURCE

State minors' consent laws. An excellent resource for state laws on minors' access to contraceptive services and other health care without parental consent is the Guttmacher Institute (www.guttmacher.org, phone 800-355-0244). This respected national nonprofit organization publishes a series of state fact sheets on issues and laws affecting sexual and reproductive rights, including abortion laws. It also provides monthly updates on state legislation.

School

Children between the ages of about six to 16 (depending on the state) must attend school. Parents can pick the school, though: Public school, private school, and homeschooling can all satisfy the legal requirement of school attendance.

States generally make rules on curriculum, special education, testing requirements, and discrimination and harassment. There are fewer federal laws about education, but some important ones, such as the No Child Left Behind Act, significantly affect how much federal money a school district receives. There are also important federal laws governing special education. (See "Educating Children With Special Needs," below.)

In most states, local school boards are responsible for day-to-day management of, as well as compliance with federal and state rules for, public schools. They supervise schools within their districts, make annual operating budgets, and hire and fire staff.

School Authority to Regulate and Discipline

Public school boards often set local rules on topics such as district transfers, dress codes, drug and alcohol testing at school dances, locker searches, and grounds for student suspension or expulsion. Schools are increasingly coming down hard on kids who bully or harass other students (see "Bullying and Harassment," above).

Over time, students and parents have challenged many rules and procedures employed by state schools. Whether a particular policy or rule is legal varies from state to state and depends heavily on the facts of each situation. For example, the U.S. Supreme Court held in 1985 that schools are subject to the Fourth Amendment and that students have a legitimate expectation of privacy. But the school has an equally legitimate need to maintain an environment in which learning can take place. For this reason, school officials need not obtain a warrant before conducting a search (of a locker, for example), nor need they have "probable cause" before searching. Instead, the search must be reasonable, under all of the circumstances.

Not all states follow the federal rule, however. Individual states may give students heightened privacy rights in this and other areas. For example, federal law permits random drug testing for student athletes, but in the state of Washington, such a policy is against the state's guarantee of protection from unreasonable searches and seizures.

Whether a particular rule or policy will pass federal and state constitutional muster is often a very tricky question. Parents and students who are concerned about the intrusiveness of a particular procedure will almost always need the help of an experienced First Amendment or criminal defense attorney.

RESOURCE

Information on school choices and rules. To find rules for your child's school, contact your local school board. You'll find a wealth of information at your state department of education website, such as requirements regarding compulsory attendance and homeschooling. If you want to check out federal laws affecting schools, such as the No Child Left Behind Act, which sets testing requirements and accountability standards, see the U.S. Department of Education website at www.ed.gov. This federal government site is also a good place to find state profiles and statistics on schools in your state. Finally, the National School

Boards Association (www.nsba.org) has extensive information in its "School Law" section on the latest topics, such as school safety and student rights.

Educating Children With Special Needs

Children with disabilities and their parents have important legal rights when it comes to education. The federal Individuals with Disabilities Education Act (IDEA) gives families of special education children the right to:

- have their child assessed or tested to determine special education eligibility and needs for specific programs and services
- inspect and review school records relating to their child
- attend an annual "individualized education program" (IEP) meeting and develop a written IEP plan for the child with representatives of the local school district, and
- resolve disputes with the school district through an impartial administrative and legal process.

IDEA defines children with disabilities as individuals between the ages of three and 22 with one or more of the following conditions: mental retardation, deafness or another hearing impairment, speech or language impairment, blindness or another visual impairment, serious emotional disturbance, orthopedic impairment, autism, traumatic brain injury, specific learning disability, or, another health impairment.

For a child to qualify for special education under IDEA, it is not enough to have one of these disabilities. There must also be evidence that the disability adversely affects the child's educational performance.

Once a child is found eligible for special education, subsequent evaluations take place at least every three years. If parents are not satisfied with the initial evaluation or feel the child's disability or special education needs have changed, they are entitled to more frequent assessments, and even outside or independent assessments.

RESOURCE

More information on IEPs and special education law. The Special Education & IEP section of www.nolo.com contains useful articles. Nolo also publishes two books on the subject, both by Lawrence Siegel: *The Complete IEP Guide: How to Advocate for Your Special Ed Child*, and *Nolo's IEP Guide: Learning Disabilities*. See www.nolo.com for each book's table of contents and sample chapter. Both books include state-by-state resources on special education. For detailed information on state and federal special education law and programs, see www.wrightslaw.com. For resources focused on learning disabilities and attention deficit hyperactivity disorder (ADHD), see LD Online at www.ldonline.org.

Children at Work

Federal and state laws seek to protect younger workers by restricting the type of work they can do and the number of hours they can work in a day. The Fair Labor Standards Act, which governs child labor, affects nearly all employers and businesses (with a few exceptions, including small farms). Some state laws are even stricter.

Types of Work

Under federal law, anyone 18 or older may work at any job, hazardous or not. Younger folks, however, face special restrictions:

- **Teenagers who are at least 17 years old** may get jobs that involve driving on public roads, if they have valid driver's licenses and no moving violations (other restrictions apply, too).
- **16- and 17-year-old teens** may perform any nonhazardous job. Jobs that are considered hazardous involve mining, wrecking and demolition, logging, and roofing, among other things.
- **14- and 15-year-old teens** may work in various nonmanufacturing, nonmining, and nonhazardous jobs, with some restrictions. They may not do construction or work as ride operators at amusement parks or in certain cooking or baking jobs. Fourteen-year-olds may not lifeguard, but a 15-year-old may if properly certified as a lifeguard at a traditional swimming pool or water amusement park.

Days and Hours of Work

Younger teens, ages 14 and 15, cannot work more than three hours on a school day, 18 hours in a school week, eight hours on a nonschool day, or 40 hours in a nonschool week. Also, the work cannot begin before 7 a.m. or end after 7 p.m.,

except from June 1 through Labor Day, when evening hours
are extended to 9 p.m.

Exceptions

Some industries have special exemptions from child labor
restrictions. For example, youths of any age may deliver
newspapers or perform in movies or plays.

Also, people who own or operate a farm or another type of
agricultural business may hire their own children, of any age,
to do any kind of work on the farm.

Other farm owners or agricultural businesses may hire a
worker who is:

- 16 years or older for any work, whether hazardous or not
- 14 or 15 years old for any nonhazardous work outside of
  school hours
- 12 or 13 years old for any nonhazardous work outside of
  school hours if the child's parents work on the same farm
  or if the parents have given their written consent, and
- ten or 11 years old if the farm has been granted a
  waiver by the U.S. Department of Labor to employ the
  youngster as a hand-harvest laborer for no more than
  eight weeks in any calendar year.

RESOURCE

Federal and state child labor rules. The U.S.
Department of Labor website, www.dol.gov (see the "Youth
& Labor" section), provides information on federal labor laws
affecting minors (or you can call 866-4-USA-DOL). State laws may

be more protective. To find yours, see the list of state departments of labor at www.dol.gov/whd/contacts/state_of.htm.

Teens and Taxes

Many teen workers will have some taxes withheld from their paychecks, even if the employment lasts for only a few months. Teens, like other employees, must complete all relevant IRS forms, including a W-4 form (*Employee's Withholding Allowance Certificate*) for every job held. Tax forms are available on the Internal Revenue Service website, www.irs.gov.

Encourage your teen to file a tax return; that way you'll ensure that they don't pay taxes unnecessarily. Most teen workers will get some, if not all, their withheld taxes refunded by filing a return.

Many teen jobs—waiting tables, for example—involve tips. Tips are taxable and need to be reported as income, so encourage your teen to keep a log of all tips received, including any share of tips that are split with other workers. Keeping a record will ensure that your teen doesn't get taxed on the basis of the employer's estimate of tips, which will usually be higher than what your child actually received.

To learn more about filing taxes, see articles in the Taxes section of www.nolo.com. For tax forms and instructions see www.irs.gov.

Work Permits for Teens

Most states require teens (the age varies by state) to get a work permit. Applications for work permits, also known as employment certificates, are typically available from a school guidance counselor.

Juvenile Crime

When a juvenile is suspected of committing a crime, the procedure that's followed is very different from that used for adults. All states have special juvenile court systems for minors who get into trouble with the law. And although some minors are ultimately judged to be delinquent by these juvenile courts, the players in a typical juvenile case—including police officers, prosecutors, and judges—have broad discretion to fashion a range of outcomes. Although the procedure for juvenile delinquency cases varies from state to state, here is a rundown of a typical juvenile case.

Laws Aimed at Kids

Many local ordinances, even if they are not age specific, have a special impact on children. Examples include restrictions on using cell phones or texting while driving, setting off fireworks, painting graffiti on someone else's property or committing other acts of vandalism, blasting loud music while driving, and acting rowdy at a sporting event. In addition, many communities set curfews for minors, limiting when they may be out late at night without a valid reason. Penalties for violating local ordinances may range from fines to community service or even jail time. To check local rules and ordinances, search the name of your county, city, or town, or check out www.statelocalgov.net, which links to the websites of many cities and counties. Or you can call your city manager's or mayor's office for this information.

Eligibility for Juvenile Court

Most cases involving young people up to 18 years of age (usually called minors or juveniles in this context) are adjudicated in juvenile court. In certain serious cases, such as murder, juveniles can be tried in adult criminal court, especially if they have lengthy juvenile court records.

Crimes Committed by Young Children and Preteens

Our legal system is based on the idea that people should be punished only when they have acted with an intent or purpose that makes them morally blameworthy. Based on this principle (known as *mens rea* or guilty state of mind), most states consider children younger than seven to be legally incapable of forming the state of mind necessary to be morally blameworthy or subject to criminal punishment. As a result, children under age seven are almost never charged with crimes. But if a very young child does cause injury or damage, the parents are on the hook to compensate the victim. In some cases, a court might even conclude that the parents' neglect led to the child's bad behavior and place the child with relatives or foster parents.

Children between the ages of seven and 14 occupy a middle ground. They are often presumed to be incapable of forming the guilty mind necessary for criminal punishment. But if a prosecutor is able to show otherwise, the child can be criminally punished.

Once minors reach age 14, most states regard them as fully capable of forming a guilty mind, and they are usually held accountable for the crimes they commit, either in juvenile or adult court.

How Police Deal With Juveniles

Police arrest some juvenile suspects for theft, simple assault, disorderly conduct, drug possession, and other common crimes. Other kids are referred to the police by parents or school officials. Regardless of how the police get wind of a potential juvenile case, they have several options for handling the situation.

Issue a warning. A police officer can detain a minor, issue a warning against further violations, then let the minor go (perhaps meeting with parents later). This is often referred to as the "counseled and released" alternative.

Hold the minor until a parent comes. Sometimes a police officer detains a minor, issues a warning, then releases the minor to the custody of a parent or guardian.

Refer to juvenile court. In instances of serious or repeat offenses or misbehavior, an officer may place the juvenile in custody and refer the case to juvenile court.

Types of Cases Heard in Juvenile Court

Two types of cases are heard in juvenile court:

- cases involving violations that apply only to minors. Examples include truancy (skipping school), violating a city curfew, and underage drinking.
- cases involving minors who are alleged to have committed crimes that would, if they were 18 and older, land them in regular criminal court.

When Cases Go to Juvenile Court

States have juvenile court systems because they recognize that many kids who run afoul of the law can be helped by being steered in the right direction rather than punished. Minors who commit crimes often receive counseling and get to stay at home instead of going to jail.

Once a police officer refers a case to juvenile court, a prosecutor or juvenile court intake officer (often a probation officer) takes over. That person may decide to dismiss the case, handle the matter informally, or file formal charges.

In deciding how to proceed, the prosecutor or intake officer typically considers:

- the severity of the offense (serious offenses, such as robbery, rape, or murder, may be transferred to adult criminal court)
- the strength of the evidence in the case
- the juvenile's age and any prior contact with the juvenile court system
- the juvenile's history of problems at home and at school, and
- the ability of the juvenile's parents to control his or her behavior.

Parental Responsibility for a Child's Misbehavior

Parental liability is the term used to refer to parents' obligation to pay for damage done by negligent, intentional, or criminal acts of their children. Most states hold parents responsible for all malicious or willful property damage done by their children (such as graffiti), but may set dollar caps on liability. Many state laws also make parents responsible for all malicious or willful personal injuries inflicted by their children. Parental liability usually ends when the child reaches the age of majority (usually 18).

Informal Proceedings

If the prosecutor or probation officer decides to proceed informally, the minor must usually appear before a probation officer or judge. No formal charge is entered against the juvenile, but the judge or court officer will usually require that the juvenile:

- listen to a stern lecture
- attend counseling
- attend after-school classes
- compensate the victim for losses
- pay a fine
- perform community service work, or
- enter probation, a program of supervision that allows minors to remain free if they fulfill specified

conditions, such as regular counseling and community service. (A minor who violates a condition of probation may be incarcerated.)

If the judge suspects a juvenile is being abused or neglected, an investigation is possible, potentially leading to proceedings to remove the minor from the home.

Formal Proceedings

A prosecutor or probation officer who decides to proceed formally will file a petition in juvenile court. The minor is then formally charged (arraigned) in front of a juvenile court judge or referee. In some serious cases, the court may decide to send the juvenile to adult criminal court.

The court will also determine whether the minor should be detained or released until the initial hearing. In most juvenile court cases, the judge allows the minor to go home while awaiting the hearing.

If the case remains in juvenile court, one of three things may happen:

The minor enters into a plea agreement. Often, a plea agreement hinges on the juvenile's compliance with certain conditions. For example, as part of a plea deal, a juvenile may need to attend counseling, obey curfews, or reimburse the victim for losses.

The minor is sent for counseling or community service. When a judge directs a minor to complete a program (such as counseling) or perform some act (such as community service or payment of restitution), the judge keeps authority over the case. If the juvenile doesn't fulfill the obligations, the court may reinstate formal charges. (These are often called diversion programs.)

The judge holds a hearing. A juvenile trial (called an "adjudicatory hearing") is much like the criminal trial of an adult. Both sides present evidence, and attorneys argue the case. In most states, the hearing is held before a judge, not a jury. At the conclusion of the hearing, the judge will determine whether or not the juvenile is delinquent (committed the charged offense).

If the court makes a delinquency ruling, a probation officer will evaluate the juvenile, order psychological examination or diagnostic tests if necessary, then make recommendations at the disposition hearing, which is similar to a sentencing hearing in adult criminal court. The judge then decides what is in the best interest of the juvenile and may order a combination of any number of things, including: counseling; placement with someone other than the parents, such as a relative or foster care; confinement in a juvenile detention facility; reimbursement of the victim; or probation. The judge may also order the juvenile to appear in court periodically (called postdisposition hearings) in order to monitor the juvenile's behavior and progress.

Sealing Juvenile Court Records

Most states let people seal (expunge) records of certain juvenile offenses. Essentially, this wipes past offenses off the books, and it is as if the juvenile court proceedings never took place. Some states automatically seal certain types of juvenile records after the offender reaches a certain age. But in most places, records are not sealed unless the offender pays a fee and files an official request (petition) with the juvenile court clerk in the county where the offense occurred.

Which juvenile records may be sealed? It varies from state to state. Usually, whether or not a record can be sealed depends on several factors.

Age. The person seeking the sealing must be an adult. In most states, this means the person making the request must be at least 18 years old.

When the offense was committed. Often, a juvenile record cannot be sealed until five years have passed from the date of the offense or from the end of the juvenile court proceedings.

Type of offense. Some states limit the types of offenses that can be expunged from a juvenile record. Many states don't allow people to expunge serious juvenile offenses—such as a violation that would be a felony in adult criminal court.

Subsequent arrests or convictions. In many states, if the person asking for expungement of a juvenile record has later criminal arrests or convictions as an adult, the request to seal the juvenile record will be denied.

If the court approves the petition and seals the juvenile records, the court then treats the juvenile court proceedings as if they never occurred. In most states, this means that if former offenders are asked whether they have a juvenile offense history, they can legally say "No." Likewise, if an employer, educational institution, government agency, or another entity does a background check, the juvenile court history will not come up. So, having a juvenile record sealed can have tremendous advantages to someone applying for a job or professional license or in any other situation that might involve inquiries about criminal history.

Sealing is not absolute, however. In certain circumstances, an expunged juvenile record may be accessible, for example, if someone applies for a job with a law enforcement agency. If a juvenile record contains a vehicle-related violation, an insurance company may be able to access a record of that offense when considering a car insurance application. Finally, juvenile offenses that are expunged from a record may still be used to increase the severity of a sentence that's handed down after a later juvenile offense or adult criminal conviction. And it must be said that, in this age of computers and online databases, even a properly sealed record often remains accessible to anyone with enough ingenuity to look long and hard through the ether.

RESOURCE

More information about juvenile court. For federal and state resources on the juvenile justice system, see the websites for the Office of Juvenile Justice and Delinquency Prevention in the U.S. Department of Justice (www.ojjdp.gov) and the National Center for Juvenile Justice (www.ncjj.org).

See *The Criminal Law Handbook: Know Your Rights, Survive the System,* by Paul Bergman and Sara J. Berman (Nolo), for more about the rights of minors in juvenile proceedings and how to help if your child gets in trouble with the law. See www.nolo.com for a sample chapter and full table of contents.

When Does a Child Become an Adult?

All the special rules that restrict and protect children cease to apply when a child reaches adulthood, or what's called the age of majority. In certain circumstances, a child may be legally emancipated before reaching the age of majority.

The Age of Majority

In most states, the age of majority is 18. At 18, you can vote, make a will, enter into binding contracts (such as to buy a house), enlist in the armed forces, and make your own decisions (without parental consent) regarding finances, medical care, and employment. A few adult rights and responsibilities, however, come later than the age of majority—notably drinking alcohol, which no state allows for anyone under age 21.

Emancipation of Minors

A minor who is "emancipated" assumes most adult responsibilities, free from parental control or support, before reaching the age of majority. Eligibility depends on state law, but usually minors can be emancipated by:

- getting married (as long as they comply with state marriage requirements, covered in Chapter 1)
- joining the military (because military policies require enlistees to have a high school diploma or GED, most young people are at least 17 or 18 before they become emancipated through enlistment), or

- getting a court order (see "Emancipation by Court Permission," below).

A few states and territories (for example, Louisiana and Puerto Rico) allow a fourth form of limited emancipation that requires only parental consent, not the court's permission.

Parents may not unilaterally declare their child emancipated, and a child cannot decide, alone, to become emancipated—for example, by running away from home. Instead, parents must support their children until the children reach adulthood—and longer if a child is disabled.

Emancipated minors are not under the care and control of parents and may function as adults in society. An emancipated minor can keep earnings from a job, sign contracts like leases, sue or be sued in court, decide where to live or attend school, make his or her own medical decisions, and more.

Most states place some limits on what an emancipated minor can do. For example, many states don't allow emancipated minors to get married without parental consent, quit school before age 16 (or whatever age the state allows), buy or drink alcohol, or vote or get a driver's license before the legal age at which other minors are allowed to.

Emancipation by Court Permission

Some (but not all) states allow a minor to be emancipated by court order. Usually, the minor must be at least 16 years old—although in California, minors as young as 14 may petition the court for emancipation. The court will grant emancipation if it believes that it's in the young person's best interest. That determination is typically based on factors such as whether the minor is:

- financially self-sufficient (usually through employment, as opposed to government aid or welfare)
- currently living apart from parents or guardians or has made alternative living arrangements
- sufficiently mature to make decisions and to function as an adult, and
- going to school or has received a high school diploma.

Minors who are seeking emancipation through a court order must follow the procedures that are set out by their state's law. Though the process varies from state to state, here's what the court procedure typically looks like:

- **Petition.** The emancipation petition must be filed by the minor (or by an attorney on the minor's behalf). Usually, the petition includes an explanation of why the minor is seeking emancipation, information about the minor's current living situation, and evidence that the minor is or soon will be financially self-sufficient.
- **Notification of parents.** In most states, minors must notify their parents or legal guardians that a petition for emancipation has been filed—or explain to the court why they do not want to do so.
- **Hearing.** In most cases, the court schedules a hearing, at which the judge asks questions and hears evidence to decide whether emancipation is in the minor's best interest.
- **Declaration of emancipation.** If the court decides that emancipation should be ordered, it will issue a Declaration of Emancipation, which the newly emancipated minor

must give to schools, doctors, landlords, and provide in any other situation that would normally require parental consent.

Alternatives to Emancipation

There are many reasons why a young person might seek emancipation. A minor who is very wealthy (a child actor, for example) might seek emancipation for financial and tax reasons. Some young people who are physically or emotionally abused want to get away from a bad home environment. Others just cannot get along with their parents or guardians. Emancipation is just one option in these situations. Other avenues to explore include getting help from government or private agencies, such as child protective services; getting family counseling or arranging mediation for everyone involved; living with another responsible adult or living away from home with the informal consent of parents.

Elder Care

Americans are living longer and healthier lives than at any time in history. Many older people just need help with daily activities in their own homes, but some require ongoing, long-term care. Whether you are thinking about your own future or seeking care for a relative who needs help (now or down the road), you have many options to consider, including how you will finance the care.

Finding At-Home or Long-Term Residential Care

Arranging long-term care for yourself or a senior relative can be extremely difficult. Here's an overview of some of your options.

At-Home Care

Lots of older people don't need medical or nursing care, but could use help with day-to-day activities. Fortunately, more and more options are available for people who want to "age in place," as staying in one's home is sometimes called. See the AARP website, www.aarp.org, for several useful articles on the subject.

The term "home care" encompasses a multitude of medical and personal services provided at home to an elder. These services often make it possible for an older person to remain at home or with a relative. Depending on what is available in your community, home care and related supplemental services can include: health care, such as monitoring a chronic health condition; personal care, such as assistance with personal hygiene; nutrition, such as meal delivery; housekeeping; social needs; transportation services; and safety, especially for people with dementia or other cognitive impairment, including making sure that the person does not become lost, disoriented, or injured.

Home care needs may be filled by community agencies or organizations, adult day care or senior centers, individuals hired through informal networks or a certified home care agency, and family and friends. Geriatric care managers can be especially helpful if you want to arrange care for an elderly relative who doesn't live nearby. A geriatric care manager will assess long-term care needs of an elderly person and organize appropriate services, including in-home care and supporting services from various providers.

RESOURCE

More on geriatric care managers. The National Association of Professional Geriatric Care Managers, www. caremanager.org, offers referrals and information about caregivers and how a geriatric care manager can help.

Finding Good Home Care

Many people hire one or more individuals to take care of an older relative. The best way to find a good home care worker is by referral. Ask your family physician about getting in-home help, or see whether your local hospital has a registry of visiting nurses. Your local Area Office on Aging (find yours at www.aoa.gov) can also provide referrals for reputable home care services, as can the Eldercare Locator (see www.eldercare.gov or call 800-677-1116). And don't forget to ask family, friends, and neighbors for referrals. Most of all, you want someone you can trust.

Anyone providing medical care must be licensed or certified by your state's home care licensing agency. So when you need medical or nursing care—not just assistance with daily activities—you should seek help from certified agencies rather than independent caregivers.

If you need nonmedical care, you can hire an independent caregiver or an agency—the caregiver does not need to be licensed or certified. But it is very important to check references carefully and to find out what credentials a potential caregiver has. For example, ask whether the caregiver has had CPR and first aid training or any other health care training. Also, be sure to define the tasks that you need the caregiver to perform, such as shopping and meal preparation, bathing and personal care, and light housekeeping, and make sure that the person is willing and able to do them.

If you hire someone directly, not through an agency, you'll need to comply with federal and state employment laws, such as verifying the legal status of the caregiver and withholding taxes from paychecks (see your state department of labor for your rules). You'll also need a plan for who will step in when the caregiver gets sick or takes time off.

Cost of In-Home Care

The cost of nonmedical home care averages $15 to $30 per hour or more, depending upon the amount of time a caregiver works each day, whether or not they live in, their skills, and other factors. A nurse practitioner or registered nurse will be much more expensive than someone who is providing nonmedical home care. If a doctor prescribes medically necessary home health care for a homebound senior, Medicare will cover some of the costs if you use a Medicare-approved home health agency. Medicare will not, however, pay for a caregiver who provides nonmedical assistance.

Assisted Living

Assisted living is the fastest growing type of senior residence. It meets the needs of millions of seniors who don't need nursing care but do want help with housekeeping and other chores and who enjoy the meals, activities, and socializing that a well-run assisted living residence provides.

Assisted living offers extensive personal assistance and services, which are not offered by independent living residences and would be extremely expensive if arranged through home care. Residents maintain the privacy and independence that are lost in more institutional, and more expensive, nursing facilities.

Typically, people in assisted living rent their own room or small apartment. It may be equipped with an emergency call system, so help can always be summoned quickly. Residents can choose from a range of services, typically including:

- domestic services, including meals and housekeeping
- assistance with personal care and the activities of daily living, but not nursing care, and
- close monitoring to help ensure their health and safety, such as keeping track of and helping a resident take the correct dose of medications or helping a resident with self-administered health aids, such as prostheses and oxygen.

Assisted living facilities range widely in cost, from $1,500 to $5,000 per month or more, depending on the size of the living space and the services provided. The cost is generally one-third to one-half the cost of a nursing facility of the same quality in the same area. In some states, Medicaid covers the cost of assisted living, although not all assisted living facilities accept payment from Medicaid.

Long-Term Residential Care

Some seniors are too ill or frail to live at home or in an assisted living residence. They need the 24-hour monitoring, extensive personal help, and nursing care that can be found only in a residential care facility.

Several types of care are available in long-term residential facilities. Skilled nursing facilities provide short-term, intensive medical care and monitoring for people recovering from acute illness or injury. Other facilities—called nursing homes, board and care homes, sheltered care homes, or something similar—provide custodial care, long-term room and board, and 24-hour assistance with personal care and other health care monitoring, but not intensive medical treatment or daily nursing. Some facilities provide only one level of care (skilled or custodial), while others offer several levels at the same location.

For someone with severe physical or mental limitations, especially Alzheimer's and other conditions that involve memory loss or dementia, it is crucial to find a facility that provides the kind of attention and care that meets the individual's specific needs. For people who need little actual nursing care, the task is to find a facility that provides physical, mental, and social stimulation, not just bed and board.

Finding a Good Residential Care Facility

The best way to find a good, affordable facility is usually to ask for referrals. Here are some good places to start:

- relatives, friends, and neighbors who have experience with a long-term care facility or know someone who does
- doctors (including your older relative's) who have personal experience with facilities in your area
- the hospital discharge planner, if your loved one is going straight from a hospital to a long-term care facility
- organizations focusing on your older relative's specific illness or disability, such as the American Heart Association, the American Cancer Society, the American Diabetes Association, or the Alzheimer's Disease Foundation
- national long-term care organizations, such Leading Age (www.leadingage.org)
- government agencies, such as your state Area Agency on Aging (find yours at www.aoa.gov), and

- church, ethnic, or fraternal organizations that may be affiliated with a particular facility or whose members may have recommendations.

See the list of resources below for organizations that provide referrals to and advice on choosing a nursing home or long-term care facility.

Paying for Residential Facility Care

Residential care is expensive. There is, however, a significant range in nursing home and other residential facility costs, depending on location, size, and facilities.

Skilled nursing facilities run between $300 and $500 per day, but, fortunately, stays there are usually relatively short, and Medicare or private health insurance will usually pick up much of the tab. To be covered by Medicare, you must receive the services from a Medicare-certified skilled nursing home after a qualifying hospital stay. (Generally, a stay of at least three days is required.)

Long-term custodial care—the kind that may last for years—costs several hundred dollars per day. Neither Medicare nor medigap private insurance supplements pay any of the cost. Medicaid will pay the full cost of custodial nursing facility care for people with low income and few assets. Eligibility varies by state; check your state's requirements to find out whether you are eligible. Medicaid will pay only for nursing home care provided in a facility certified by the government to provide service to Medicaid recipients. Long-term care insurance, also known as nursing home insurance, will pay for this type of care if you're one of the small percentage of people who have that type of insurance.

> **RESOURCE**
>
> **More on choosing at-home and long-term care:**

- **Eldercare Locator,** www.eldercare.gov, phone 800-677-1116, a program of the U.S. Administration on Aging, provides a wide variety of resources, including caregivers, health insurance, long-term care, in-home services, elder abuse prevention, transportation, nursing homes, and more.

- **Nolo's Long-Term Care section,** www.nolo.com/legal-encyclopedia/long-term-care, explains how to find the right long-term care (in-home, assisted living, or nursing home) at the right price, and includes articles on topics such as long-term care insurance.

- *Long-Term Care: How to Plan & Pay for It,* by Joseph Matthews (Nolo), explains the full range of options from in-home care to nursing homes with detailed advice on how to find the best care you can afford. See www.nolo.com for a sample chapter and full table of contents.

- **The State Health Insurance Assistance Program (SHIP),** in your state (www.shiptalk.org) provides counselors who can review your existing coverage and find any government programs that may help with your health insurance and long-term care expenses.

- **Leading Age,** www.leadingage.org, provides information about member residential facilities.

- **Medicare,** www.medicare.gov/nursinghomecompare, offers a user-friendly checklist on choosing long-term care, as well as summaries of the types of long-term care that are available in your area, comparisons of financing options, and advice on finding and evaluating the quality of nursing homes. The site also provides links to counseling and assistance resources for more long-term care information.

- **Administration on Aging,** www.aoa.gov (phone 202-401-4634), is a federal government clearinghouse for a broad array of information of interest to elders and their families, including your state Area Agency on Aging.

- **www.longtermcare.gov** provides information and resources to help consumers plan for long-term care needs.

- **www.careconversations.org** provides information on nursing homes, assisted living facilities, residential care, and other types of long-term care, plus helpful tips on coping with the transition of a family member into an assisted living residence, caring for someone with Alzheimer's, and writing an advance directive.

- **The National Consumer Voice for Quality Long-Term Care,** www.theconsumervoice.org, provides state and local resources for residents or family members advocating for quality long-term care, and consumer fact sheets with information on federally guaranteed residents' rights, selecting a nursing home, forming family councils, and more.

- **AARP,** www.aarp.org, has a "Caregiving" section in the Home & Family area of its site that provides useful consumer information on long-term care options.

- **Family Caregiver Alliance,** www.caregiver.org, provides advice and support for caregivers and referrals to local government, nonprofit, and private programs of interest to caregivers and the recipients of long-term care.

- **www.caring.com** provides information, support, and referrals for people who care for aging parents, spouses, and other loved ones.

Medicare and Medicaid

Medicare and Medicaid have similar names, and both can help with medical expenses, but they are two very different programs:

- **Medicaid** is for low-income, financially needy people.
- **Medicare** is not tied to individual need; instead, eligibility is based primarily on age and work history.

Although you may qualify for and receive coverage from both Medicare and Medicaid, there are separate eligibility requirements for each program. Being eligible for one program does not mean you are eligible for the other.

Medicare

This federal program was created to deal with the high medical costs that older people face—especially troublesome given the reduced earning power of retired people. But your actual need is irrelevant when it comes to eligibility. You are entitled to Medicare not because you can't pay for medical services but because you or your spouse paid for it through your taxes.

Generally, if you are 65 or older and paid Medicare taxes for at least ten years, you will qualify for Medicare Part A, which helps cover the costs of care in a hospital or skilled nursing facility. If you didn't pay Medicare taxes for that long, you can buy Part A coverage. You may apply for coverage by calling the Social Security Administration or going to your local office.

Medicare doesn't pay for everything, and so many Medicare recipients aged 65 or over buy what's called "medigap" insurance. That's insurance that's designed to pay health care bills not covered by Medicare, such as deductibles.

Other Medicare recipients join Medicare managed care plans to cover costs not covered by traditional Medicare.

> ## ! CAUTION
>
> **Read the fine print.** Before buying a medigap insurance policy, consider not only the services covered (long-term custodial care is not), but the amount of benefits, the monthly cost of the policy, how much premiums may rise, and renewal policies. The Medicare website (www.medicare.gov) has useful articles on choosing medigap insurance.

Medicaid

Medicaid is set up by the federal government and administered differently in each state. This program goes by different names in some states; for example, it's called MassHealth in Massachusetts and Medi-Cal in California.

If you qualify for both Medicare and Medicaid, Medicaid will pay for most Medicare Part A and B premiums, deductibles, and co-payments.

RESOURCE

More on Medicare and Medicaid:

- **Nolo's Medicare & Medicaid section,** www.nolo.com/
legal-encyclopedia/medicare-medicaid, provides easy-
to-understand information about choosing a Medicare
managed care plan, using medigap to fill in gaps in your
Medicare coverage, how Medicare Parts A and B work,
and whether and when to enroll in Medicare Part D,
Prescription Drug Coverage.

- *Social Security, Medicare & Government Pensions: Get
the Most Out of Your Retirement & Medical Benefits,* by
Joseph L. Matthews (Nolo), provides extensive advice on
Medicaid, medigap insurance, Medicare, and Medicare
managed care plans. See www.nolo.com for a sample
chapter and full table of contents.

- **The official U.S. government Medicare site,** www.
medicare.gov, provides forms to apply for Medicare and
help choosing a policy to supplement Medicare coverage,
finding doctors, and much more. You can also call
800-MEDICARE for questions regarding billing and claims.

- **The Social Security Administration's website,** www.ssa.gov/
pgm/medicare.htm, contains a wealth of information about
Medicare benefits, applying for benefits, and information
about Medicare prescription drug plan costs.

- **The Centers for Medicare & Medicaid Services' website,**
www.cms.gov, has lots of research and data about how
these programs are administered and who receives benefits.

Comparing Medicare and Medicaid

	Medicare	Medicaid
Who is eligible	Medicare covers almost everyone 65 or older, people on Social Security disability, and some people with permanent kidney failure.	Medicaid covers low-income and financially needy people, including those over 65 who are also on Medicare.
Who administers the program	Medicare is a federal program whose rules are the same all over the country. Medicare information is available at your Social Security office.	Medicaid is administered by each state; rules differ in each state. Get information at your county social services, welfare, or department of human services office.
What it covers	Medicare hospital insurance (Part A) provides basic coverage for hospital stays and posthospital nursing facility and home health care. Medicare medical insurance (Part B) pays most basic doctor and laboratory costs and some outpatient medical services, including medical equipment and supplies, home health care, and physical therapy. Medicare prescription drug coverage (Part D) pays some of the costs of prescription medications.	Medicaid provides comprehensive inpatient and outpatient health care coverage, including many services and costs. Medicaid does not cover prescription drugs, diagnostic care, or eyeglasses. The amount of coverage, however, varies from state to state. Medicaid can pay Medicare deductibles and the 20% portion of charges not paid by Medicare. Medicaid can also pay the Medicare premium.

Comparing Medicare and Medicaid, continued		
	Medicare	**Medicaid**
How much you pay	You pay a yearly deductible for both Medicare Part A and Part B, and make hefty co-payments for extended hospital stays.	In some states, Medicaid charges consumers small amounts for certain services.
	Under Part B, you pay the 20% of doctors' bills Medicare does not pay, and sometimes up to 15% more. Part B also charges a monthly premium. Under Part D, you pay a monthly premium, a deductible, co-payments, and all of your prescription drug costs over a certain yearly amount and up to a ceiling amount, unless you qualify for a low-income subsidy.	

Long-Term Care Insurance

Long-term care (LTC) insurance, also known as nursing home insurance, is widely advertised as protection against the costs of long-term care, particularly residential nursing facilities. However, this kind of insurance is expensive, and it often provides only limited benefits—with many restrictions and conditions—that may end up covering only a small percentage, or nothing at all, of total long-term care costs.

Insurance companies market long-term care (LTC) insurance by suggesting that consumers are likely to wind up spending years in a nursing facility—a prospect that would wipe out their savings and perhaps leave them without a roof over their heads. However, the actual odds of a long nursing facility stay are considerably lower than the insurance industry would like you to imagine, and with the protection afforded by Medicaid laws, there is little risk of being thrown out of a nursing facility and into the street.

When you consider the true odds of a long nursing facility stay along with the high cost of LTC insurance and the other things you could do with that premium money, you may find that for you—as for the 95% of the population over age 65 who have not invested in it—LTC insurance is not a good bet.

If you are considering LTC insurance, be a very careful consumer. Comparison shop among several policies, checking each for exclusions and limitations. Don't base your decision solely on advice from an insurance agent or broker who is trying to sell you a policy. Check out state-certified (called "state-partnership") long-term care insurance policies, which offer some of the best terms available.

RESOURCE

More on long-term care insurance. Check *Consumer Reports* magazine at www.consumerreports.org, for their latest analysis of LTC insurance policies, and the website, www.longtermcare.gov, for useful advice, including average costs of LTC insurance in your area.

Health Care Directives and Power of Attorney Forms

The time may come when you or loved ones will need to make financial and health care decisions for an older relative. It's a good idea to have documents giving you the legal authority you need to do so. These include:

- A **durable power of attorney for health care**, which names a trusted person to make health care decisions for you if you can't or don't want to.
- An **advance medical directive**, also known as a living will or declaration, which lets you spell out your wishes for end-of-life care. In some states, this may be combined in a single form with a durable power of attorney for health care, in which case it's commonly called an advance health care directive.
- A **durable power of attorney for finances**, which lets you give someone else authority to handle your financial matters (this can be drafted so that it goes into effect as soon as it's signed or only if you become incapacitated).

RESOURCE

Health care directives and financial power of attorney forms. You can create these forms, in addition to a will and other important estate planning documents, using *Quicken WillMaker Plus* (software published by Nolo).

Conservatorships and Adult Guardianships

If a family member is already incapacitated and didn't sign durable powers of attorney for finances and health care in advance, you may need to ask a court for authority over your loved one's finances and personal affairs—that is, to name you as conservator or guardian. Generally, conservatorships are established for people who are in comas, suffer from severe dementia, or have other serious illnesses or injuries. Court proceedings to establish conservatorships are expensive, time-consuming, and public—not what a family member wants when dealing with a crisis involving a family member. Conservators are subject to court supervision, which is designed to safeguard the incapacitated adult's property and welfare. Conservators must act until the court issues an order ending the conservatorship (this ordinarily happens when the incapacitated person dies or no longer needs this level of assistance).

RESOURCE

More on conservatorships and guardians.
See www.nolo.com/legal-encyclopedia/conservatorships-adult-guardianships-30063.html for more information on this subject.

Index

A

⚖ NOLO   *Online Legal Forms*

Nolo offers a large library of legal solutions and forms, created by Nolo's in-house legal staff. These reliable documents can be prepared in minutes.

Create a Document

- **Incorporation.** Incorporate your business in any state.
- **LLC Formations.** Gain asset protection and pass-through tax status in any state.
- **Wills.** Nolo has helped people make over 2 million wills. Is it time to make or revise yours?
- **Living Trust (avoid probate).** Plan now to save your family the cost, delays, and hassle of probate.
- **Trademark.** Protect the name of your business or product.
- **Provisional Patent.** Preserve your rights under patent law and claim "patent pending" status.

Download a Legal Form

Nolo.com has hundreds of top quality legal forms available for download—bills of sale, promissory notes, nondisclosure agreements, LLC operating agreements, corporate minutes, commercial lease, motor vehicle bill of sale, consignment agreements and many more.

Review Your Documents

Many lawyers in Nolo's consumer-friendly lawyer directory will review Nolo documents for a very reasonable fee. Check their detailed profiles at **Nolo.com/lawyers**.

On Nolo.com you'll also find:

Books & Software

Nolo publishes hundreds of great books and software programs for
consumers and business owners. Order a copy, or download an ebook
version instantly, at Nolo.com.

Online Legal Documents

You can quickly and easily make a will or living trust, form an LLC or
corporation, apply for a trademark or provisional patent, or make
hundreds of other forms—online.

Free Legal Information

Thousands of articles answer common questions about everyday
legal issues including wills, bankruptcy, small business formation,
divorce, patents, employment, and much more.

Plain-English Legal Dictionary

Stumped by jargon? Look it up in America's most up-to-date
source for definitions of legal terms, free at nolo.com.

Lawyer Directory

Nolo's consumer-friendly lawyer directory provides in-depth profiles
of lawyers all over America. You'll find all the information you need
to choose the right lawyer.

FABQWM2